Customer SERVICE

Customer SERVICE

How to Achieve Total Customer Satisfaction

MALCOLM PEEL

Kogan Page

Ref: Copyright page

First published in 1987
First paperback edition 1988
Reprinted 1991
Reprinted with revisions 1993

Kogan Page Limited
120 Pentonville Road
London N1 9JN

British Library Cataloguing in Publication Data

A CIP record for this book is available from the British Library.

ISBN 1-85091-305-6 Pbk

Printed and bound in Great Britain by Biddles Limited, Guildford and Kings Lynn

Contents

Acknowledgements

I am not sure whether anything in this book is original; I suspect not. I know that it could not have been written without help from the work of many other writers. Those that have been of particular value to me are:

Warren Blanding, in *The Practical Handbook of Distribution/ Customer Service*, published by the Traffic Service Corporation, and also in several manuals he has produced, some with Leslie Hansen Harps.

Martin Christopher, in *Customer Service and Distribution Strategy*, with Philip Schary and Tage Skjott-Larsen, published by Halsted Press, and also in a number of articles.

Bernard J La Londe and Paul H Zinszer in *Customer Service: Meaning and Measurement*, published by the National Council of Physical Distribution Management.

Brian Moores and his contributors, in *Are they being Served?* published by Philip Allan.

I owe a debt to everyone who has told me of their own experiences as a customer, in many cases going to considerable lengths to remember and record their stories. These are:

Bob Archer, David Aston, Laurie and Betty Cooper, Dr Warwick Alan and Valerie Cooper, Captain Christopher Alan Hopkinson RN, Tony and Dorothy Lucas, Philip Moon, Dr John Nicholls, Hilary Peel, Lorna Stewart, and Jenny White.

A number of organisations kindly and patiently replied to a questionnaire, many of them adding much useful additional information. These are:

Abbey National Building Society, Barclays Bank plc, Cadbury

7

Ltd, Gateway Foodmarkets Limited, Lloyds Bank plc, London Electricity Board, Marks and Spencer plc, and J Sainsbury plc.

I would like to express special thanks to Cecil Melling and the Eastern Electricity Board for permission to reproduce the passage from his book *Light in the East* on page 30.

I am especially grateful to Bob Norton and the staff of the Management Information Centre of the Institute of Management for their invaluable help in compiling bibliographies and obtaining material for me.

At the end of the day, the brunt of the problems have been borne by my ever patient family, Nancy, Katherine and Richard, without whose understanding I could have done nothing. To Richard in particular I owe much, as he alone could fathom the customer-unfriendly ways of my word processor and its manual.

Malcolm Peel

Introduction

'The customer is King.' 'The customer is always right.' 'We put our customers first.' 'Look after your customers, and they will look after you.' ... the world is full of pious sayings about customer service.

But if there is one thing the world is even fuller of, it is of unhappy customers. Not only private customers, with a few pounds to spend, but organisational buyers with budgets of millions a year. Not only suffering from rudeness and silliness, but from gross incompetence and mismanagement of all kinds.

This is the more surprising as each of us is in turn buyer and seller, customer and supplier; we all know both roles from the inside. But somehow, we find it difficult to relate the two experiences together. Like driving on a road in the opposite direction to the one we know best, we may fail to spot that we are approaching that dangerous bend.

Whatever our organisation and whatever our role in that organisation, we will be involved in customer service, perhaps more frequently than we are aware. And the service we then give is certain to have an effect, possibly a major effect, on the success of everything the organisation is seeking to achieve.

The aim of this book is to help those who wish to improve the service they or others give to customers. It is based on the belief that customer service is not an optional extra—the icing on the cake—but central to the success or failure of every organisation. It is also based on the certainty that we can, if we wish, achieve substantial improvements in the service we give.

It suggests that the elements of customer service are essentially the same for all kinds of organisation, whether in the public or private sector, whether multinational or one-person, and whether engaged in industrial, service, professional or any other activities. It is based on the firm belief that lessons from one area can be of great relevance in others. I hope it may help everyone who is, directly or indirectly, involved in giving customer service, as a supervisor, manager, proprietor, trainer or in the front line.

Surprisingly, my research suggests that whilst the subject is widely accepted to be of great and growing importance, the practical literature available is sparse. This book does not aim to break new ground; it does try to bring the whole subject together into a comprehensive framework, and to be action-orientated and essentially practical. If it achieves this, I hope it may do something to fill an unaccountable near-void.

The Chamber of Horrors

Everyone has their supply of horror stories; all the following examples have been reported as happening within the twelve months prior to the book being written.

The country bus stop

The rain poured down, and as the young girl huddled under the tree she stared hopefully down the country road, praying silently that the morning bus would come quickly. It was already nearly a quarter of an hour behind time; much more and she would be late for work at the bank, something that was seriously frowned on. The water dripped down the collar of her raincoat, and a solitary car sprayed her as it passed on the other side.

At last, the grey shape of the bus appeared lumbering through the driving rain. Instead of stopping beside her, it continued past, splashing her, and squeaked to a halt some 15 yards down the road. As always, there was one solitary passenger inside. The girl splashed up, the driver operated the door mechanism, and leant forward as she entered. 'I'll not stop for you again if you stand there,' he said. 'The stop's here.'

The failed MOT

'Can't let you drive the car away,' said the Service Manager. 'Why ever not?' asked the owner, in alarm. 'Failed the MOT, hasn't it,' came the reply, in a tone implying utter imbecility on the part of the customer. 'But why?' 'Needs new brake pads.' 'Surely you could have fitted them?' 'None in stock.' 'But at least you could have rung me up; you've had the car since eight this morning, and you took my number.' 'We haven't time to go ringing people up, we've a job to do.' 'But however do you think I'm going to get home tonight? It's 10 miles and the last bus went quarter of an hour ago.' 'Sorry, mate, we're a garage, not a bleeding taxi service.'

The cow in the toilet

'You can't go in there!' The shout rang out across the ladies' toilet. Panic stricken, the woman turned, to find herself facing a very large cleaner, equipped with mop and zinc pail. 'Why?' she queried, hesitantly, vague images of parcel bombs or nameless diseases filling her head. 'Anyone but a complete moron could see I was just going to do that one. Why d'you think I left the door open, you stupid cow?' Seeing the mop a few inches from her nose, the traveller picked her way through the group of silent onlookers, and went in search of an alternative.

The birthday present

'Ann will get her present in good time', thought her Aunt. 'It's Friday today, and I've posted it first class; she might get it tomorrow, but it's sure to be there by Monday, and her eighteenth birthday isn't till Tuesday.' The next Friday evening, on her return from work, Ann found a printed card on her mat. It told her that an 'attempt had been made' to deliver a package at her address on Wednesday, but as there was no-one to receive it, it could now be collected from the nearest parcel office (six miles away) between the hours of nine and five, Monday to Friday only. The card was postmarked on the Thursday.

An Inspector calls

'Your electricity meter has not been read by the Board's staff for 12 months. Our Inspector will call to examine your meter next Monday,' read the printed card on the mat. 'I have to be at work on Monday,' explained the consumer on the telephone to the local office, 'and I live alone. If your man calls first thing, before nine, I can hang on for him.' 'Oh, no, we can't do that.' 'Well, if we can fix a time later in the day, I can ask my employer if he could spare me for an hour.' 'That's not possible; our Inspectors may call at any time.' 'Do you expect me to take a day's leave, then?' 'That's your concern. Under the provisions of the Act the Board has the right to see

the meter, and may cut off supply if that is denied.' The consumer
took a day's leave, but the Inspector did not appear...

The silver screen

'You can't take those cans of drink into the cinema,' announced the
attendant to the young boys. 'But we've got tickets for the film',
they replied plaintively. 'You'd better decide between that and
your cans. If you give them to me, I'll put them on one side until
you come out.' At the end of the performance, no attendant was
visible in the foyer; the boys left without their drink. Next Satur-
day, they called in, specially to pick them up. 'Can't have them;
they're locked in the manager's office, he's not here and we don't
have a key,' they were told. Their father walked across town, to be
told, without a ghost of apology, the same story. Only after heated
exchanges was the 'key to the manager's office' suddenly found,
and the cans of drink reluctantly, and still without apology,
produced.

The invisible video

'Can you repair this?' asked the man in the video repair shop. 'Yes,
sir,' replied the man at the counter, taking the video and writing
out a receipt. 'How long will it be?' 'About a couple of weeks; we'll
give you a ring when it's ready.' Three weeks later, the customer
rang the shop; they were just going to start, he was told. Ten days
after that, he rang again. There was a problem; the fitter didn't
know about that model; he had had to send off for the workshop
manual. After a further week, another call elicited the news that
the manual didn't help with such a complicated bit of equipment;
the repairers were prepared to send the model to the manufacturer's agents. If they did so, it would cost £8 postage and packing.
The agents would send an estimate. When pressed on the next
step, it was stated that if the estimate was not accepted, there
would be a charge of £15 for inspecting the equipment, plus the
cost of return post and packing. 'Of course, we don't normally
touch these models,' the customer was told. 'But you accepted it.'
'Yes, the man in the branch shouldn't have done that.' The customer asked for his machine to be returned. When he called to
collect it, he was presented with an invoice for the workshop
manual. After some clear talking, in which his solicitor was mentioned, the set was handed over, unrepaired, just six weeks after it
had been left.

How to run a railway

In the unlit train that should have left ten minutes ago, the solitary passenger walked helplessly down the carriage in search of information. On the platform, two railwaymen conversed. 'Cancelled yesterday,' one was telling the other, 'no driver.' 'Is there a driver today?' interrupted the passenger, in panic, thinking of his connection and waiting family 150 miles away. 'No idea, mate.' The two returned to their conversation. 'Who does know?' persisted the passenger, bravely. 'They might know in the box,' came back the answer, in the tones of one hurt by another's total lack of manners. 'How can we find out?' 'Not my job, mate.' 'Whose is it?' 'Search me. There's the station inspector.' 'Where is he?' 'No idea.' The two turned away. 'Could try platform one,' one muttered over his shoulder, 'or it may be his rest day. Couldn't run a railway if they tried, this lot . . . ' The two disappeared into the refreshment room.

Clip the coupon

The lady in the supermarket queue nearly fainted. Feeling in her coat pocket, she realised she had come out without her purse. Although she had only one purchase, a packet of soapflakes, her loose change fell short of the purchase price by ten pence. About to turn back and replace it on the shelves, it suddenly occurred to her that she had a coupon worth ten pence in her pocket. At the checkout, she handed across cash and coupon. 'I need another 10p, madam,' said the girl. 'But there's a coupon there worth 10p; that makes the full amount.' 'Sorry, madam, we must be paid the cash before the money can be refunded.'

The dialogue ground to a halt, the lady transfixed with disbelief. At last, someone down the queue pushed a 10p piece into her hand. 'Give her this,' she said. The girl at the checkout took the extra coin, dropped the remaining money into the open till, and handed back the lent 10p. 'Thank you, madam,' she said.

The reader can, without doubt, cap most of these experiences.

The framework of the book

The remainder of the book is in three sections:

Part 1: Definition. Chapters 1 and 2 examine what is meant by 'customer service'. They look at alternative definitions, suggest why it is now of central importance to organisations of all kinds, examine the sequence of activities which make it up, how these apply in the various sectors of economic activity, and what are the common expectations of customers everywhere.

Part 2: Person-to-person. Chapters 3 to 10 take a detailed and practical look at the interpersonal aspects of customer service. They consider service when face-to-face with the customer, through communication by the written word and the telephone, the problems of dealing with awkward customers and handling complaints, and the effect of 'hardware'—the equipment, environment and physical accompaniments which surround service.

Part 3: Management. Chapters 11 to 14 turn to the management aspects of customer service. They look at the effects of policy and organisation, systems and procedures, and then turn to the value of a customer service survey, how to conduct one, and how to develop an improvement plan.

The Top Twenty. The final pages offer a list of twenty of the action points from each chapter suggested as those likely to achieve the greatest possible improvement in the least possible time.

At the end of each chapter are lists of action points (72 points in all) and thought-starters, aimed to help the reader relate what has been said to his own experience and circumstances.

Some passages have been written in words which more naturally fit the larger organisation, but I believe that almost all can be applied to organisations of every size and in every sector. Indeed, I very much hope that the exercise of applying concepts to contexts other than those in whose terms they are written may prove a positive aid to creative thought.

Please read 'he or she', 'him or her' as applicable throughout. I do not intend to be sexist, as can be seen in the pronouns in the section on secretaries.

___

Thought-starters

1. What are the worst examples of customer service you have ever experienced,
   (a) as a private individual
   (b) in your working capacity?
2. What action did you take in these cases? Did you

(a) complain, and if not, why not?
(b) tell others, and if so, how many?
(c) feel guilty yourself?
(d) use the organisation concerned again, and if so, why?
3. Was there any difference between your reaction in your private or working capacity, and if so, why?
4. Try jotting down your own definition of customer service.

PART 1

DEFINITION

1
WHAT IS CUSTOMER SERVICE?

THE SERVICE GIVEN to customers has always been important. Easy interpersonal relationships, convenient and rapid delivery, and sympathetic handling of complaints, for example, have consistently given a competitive edge to suppliers whose goods were no different from those of their competitors. But there are reasons to believe that today, customer service is not only more important than ever before, but may become the principal agent of success or cause of failure for many organisations.

Organisational drive

Every organisation has its main drive; the principal reason for its existence, from which all aspects of its policy, procedures and activities spring, and which determines its culture and the attitudes of its staff at every level.

Many organisations are *product-driven*. Their motivation springs from the product they make, or the specific service they provide. Their mission is to make good widgets, or run a railway; if this also provides a living, well and good. They will tend to regard making money, or satisfying customers as less important than designing and producing. The computer software industry provides a clear example of this. Many of its products are made almost unusable by an ever-increasing clutter of unwanted features. They have the appearance of being added because someone has found a new and clever way of doing something rather than to meet customer demand. The phrase 'customer friendly' is often no more than a bad joke.

Other organisations are *profit-driven*. For them, product is relatively unimportant; they will undertake almost any activities that will make money. They will buy and sell subsidiaries, strip assets, shut facilities and terminate product lines, if the bottom line is improved. For these also, the satisfaction of the customer is a less important activity.

A few organisations appear to see themselves as *employee-driven*, in the sense that the provision of continued employment for staff, sub-contractors and others is their central purpose.

Those organisations which will succeed in the future seem likely to be those that are *customer-driven*. Unless customer satisfaction is thrust to the centre of all thinking and activity, survival must be doubtful.

The customer-driven organisation

'The purpose of a business is to create and keep a customer,' says Theodore Levitt.[1]

In an increasing number of markets, differentiation by design, quality, packaging or price has become increasingly difficult to achieve. As Peter Benton, a past Director-General of the British Institute of Management, has said, 'Products today are conduits that can be used to deliver added value to the customer.'

Supermarket chains, for example, have now realised that they have increasing difficulty in differentiating themselves from their competitors by the products they sell or the prices at which they sell them. Creating an image by advertising and public relations becomes harder and less cost-effective. But the provision of greatly improved customer service, through well-trained staff, high quality environment, good car-parking facilities, free bus services, no-quibble return of goods, efficient checkout systems, in-house catering, cashpoint and other facilities offer the option of adding what is seen by customers as greatly enhanced value and thus a competitive advantage.

Airlines that compete not by faster schedules or lower fares, but by training staff to understand and meet the needs of their travellers, are using customer service as a main weapon against their competitors.

The undergraduate who takes car-servicing facilities round the university campus to his friends, servicing their cars outside their rooms, is adding value to a basic product through superior customer service. Many small businesses are now growing bigger by the same philosophy.

Some parts of existing industry have picked up the message sooner than others, realising that customer service in all its aspects represents an extremely cost-efficient means of beating the competition—in many cases the only means available.

Management theory lagged behind in this area for many years. For example, Brech's comprehensive and much used manual *The Principles and Practice of Management* has only seven brief references to 'customer' in its 1054 pages, and none to 'customer service'. Similar comments could be made about most of the well-known texts on management written up to the last few years; customers and customer service are virtually unmentioned. However, there has been a flood of new literature on the subject since this book was first published in 1987.

This picture is now changing rapidly. In the USA in particular, the central role of the customer has been widely recognised for a number of years. In Britain, an increasing number of organisations in both public and private sectors have invested massive amounts of time and effort to put the customer in the centre of their operation.

The cost of bad customer service

There have been attempts to put a cost figure against the failure to provide good service.

Direct cost may be incurred by the effort of handling complaints, the cost of returns and refunds, the cost of legal actions, dealing with consumer-protection bodies and necessary corrective public relations. But indirect costs are likely to be far greater, and will accrue from lost sales to those directly affected, lost sales to those who are told about the failure, and above all by the cost of acquiring new customers to replace those lost.

It has been suggested that the cost of acquiring new customers can be five times greater than the cost of retaining existing customers through good service. The actual ratio must vary widely according to circumstances, and in many cases will be far higher.

Perhaps the greatest cost of all is likely to be the cost of lost opportunities to expand. The cost of these may be virtually infinite.

The many meanings of 'customer service'

There is no general agreement as to what is meant by 'customer service'. The phrase is used in at least five different ways:

1. The activities involved in ensuring that a product or service is delivered to the customer on time in the correct quantities
2. The interpersonal working relationships between the staff of a supplier and a customer
3. The provision of after-sales repair and maintenance facilities
4. The department of an organisation which handles customer complaints
5. The order-taking department of an organisation

Before trying to relate these meanings together it may be helpful to take the phrase apart, and look separately at the words 'customer' and 'service'.

'Customer'

During the business cycle, the same individual (or organisation) will pass from being a member of the 'public', through the roles of 'prospect', 'purchaser/buyer' to 'consumer/user'. The member of the 'public' is not particularly interested in the product; the 'prospect' is interested but has not yet decided to buy; the 'purchaser' or 'buyer' has just decided, and the 'consumer' or 'user' is living with the consequences of having bought.

The word 'customer' will be used to cover the same individual or organisation through this sequence from the stage of prospect to that of consumer.

The word will also be used to mean those who buy services rather than products, and who are often known by other names; 'patients' who buy health care, 'pupils' (or maybe their parents) who buy education, 'members' of clubs, institutes and professional organisations, 'clients' of solicitors, accountants and other professions, 'passengers' of passenger carriers, 'guests' of hotels and guest houses, 'diners' of restaurants and other more rare and specialised words with the same general meaning. In each of these cases, there is a customer-supplier relationship, although it may not always be thought of in that way, and the indirect method of payment through rates or taxes may sometimes make it less apparent.

The supply chain
Goods and services pass down a 'supply chain', which may sometimes be very long. From the quarrymen who dig out the ore,
through the steelmaker, those who forge components, the manufacturer who bolts them on, the agent who buys the product whole-
sale, to the end user who drives the car on the road stretches a long
and complicated chain. The chain is held together by three agencies; information, transactions involving payment, and the physical distribution of goods as in Figure 1 below.

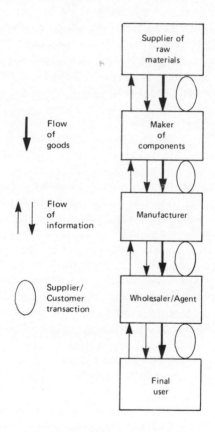

Figure 1. *The supply chain*

'Customer' is the word usually used to describe the next link down this chain. The customer of the agent, for example, is the end user, and the customer of the manufacturer is the agent. But it is also true that the ultimate user is the customer of the manufacturer, and in a weaker sense that the ultimate user is the customer of the maker of components, even of the quarryman. In the final analysis, customers buy not from a single supplier, but from a chain, each of whose links will affect the product and service he receives. If, for example, supply of the ore is delayed, the ultimate user is likely to suffer.

It is also true that every organisation is both a customer and a supplier; we cannot supply unless we have obtained input. The same is true for us as individuals; we play the role of customer, at many times and in many ways, and we also act as supplier (although many of us are suppliers of a service rather than of goods, through the sale of our labour to an employer).

Internal customers
Everyone has customers; departments and individuals in an organisation are linked together in chains of service in the same way as separate organisations.

Some of the new approaches to work now developing may result in an economy which has many more customers and suppliers. The idea of self-determining working groups, acting entrepreneurially within an organisation, and cutting across the traditional boundaries of functions, is now attracting attention. 'Networking' and 'outsourcing', by which self-employed individuals or small groups supply services to larger organisations that would traditionally have employed them, is also becoming commoner. If these trends continue, the number of customer/supplier relationships will grow greatly in the years to come.

Customers come in all shapes and sizes
Customers do not have to be nervous little old ladies or tetchy Colonel Blimps.

While retail customers must always be in the majority, our position on the supply chain may mean that most or all of our customers are professional. Customers may just as well be the canny and experienced operators in the purchasing department of a major multinational, the powerful buyers of a supermarket chain, or the dynamic owners of a thrusting software house. Superficially, the situation may sometimes seem different, but in practice the customer/supplier relationship will work in much the same way. The same technical and personal factors operate at every level, similar problems and failures occur, and similar solutions may be found.

Organisations without customers
Unless we see our organisation as having customers, we will have little interest in customer service.

The question is therefore of more than academic interest; can there be organisations without customers?

What, for example, is the situation of the armed forces? If they have 'customers', who are they? Are they the national enemies who are on the receiving end of their activity, or the taxpayer who foots the bill? What about the prison services? What is the situation of the police, customs and excise, national and local government departments and government agencies? It is ironic that the title of some of these organisations actually includes the word 'service'.

In all these cases, the relationship between those who pay and those who receive service is broken and indirect. For this reason, neither the organisation nor the public they serve usually think in terms of a customer/supplier relationship. Many of their activities, however, (including, for example, a surprising number of police activities) have clear customer service aspects. The perception of these aspects must give such organisations new insights which can only help to make their operation more effective.

'Service'
It is not so long since 'going into service' was a commonly used expression meaning becoming a domestic servant. The word 'service' still has a strong connection with 'servant' and 'servility' that most of us find repellent.

For this reason, some organisations have rejected the word 'service' in this context, and substituted 'care', as in the phrase 'customer care'. While overcoming this objection, this has the effect of narrowing the meaning, by emphasising purely behavioural aspects, which are only part of the whole. Similar expressions used which avoid the word 'service' include 'customer satisfaction' and the British Airways slogan 'customer first'.

Other common uses of the word 'service' throw in several red herrings. 'The services' means the armed forces. 'The public services' are activities essential to the social fabric but which do not contribute directly to the creation of wealth. 'Servicing' usually means the activities necessary to keep machinery in working order, but also has an agricultural meaning.

'The service sector' describes that part of the economy which generally exists to do things for its customers rather than supply goods to them; to carry them from place to place, or nurse them back to health. There are some sectors (such as catering) in which the distinction between goods and services is fine and blurred. But the relationship between supplier and customer is the same, and has the same phases, whether goods or services are supplied.

'Customer service'

Putting the two words together, we find many definitions to choose from. Some concentrate on one or other of the narrower aspects listed at the start of this chapter. One of the most succinct and useful is that of the American writer on customer service, Frances Gaither Tucker,[2] who speaks of 'All activities which bind a corporation to its customers'.

This emphasises that customer service is a range of activities that together establish a relationship; as such it will include everything that is separately described in the five definitions listed earlier in this chapter and more besides. The only objection to this definition may be that it is too inclusive, and would embrace selling, public relations and publicity, which seem to be separate activities in their own right and which may sometimes even be in conflict with customer service.

There is no virtue in creating further definitions for their own sake, but the following is suggested as including certain features which may be of practical value:

 Secondary activities undertaken by an organisation to maximise customer satisfaction in its primary activities.

The primary activities of an organisation will include supplying goods or services, and the design, marketing, selling, purchasing, assembly, manufacturing and accountancy that go with this.

The primary activities of a car manufacturer, for example, are to design, make and sell cars. The primary activities of a restaurant are the cooking and selling of meals to diners. The primary activities of a bus operator are the operation of buses on which passengers pay to travel.

Some writers on customer service speak of 'technical' and 'expressive' activities with generally similar meanings to what we describe as primary and secondary activities.

Customer service activities

These secondary, or customer service activities include some which are special to customer service, and some which are intimately related to primary activities. The special activities are in the areas of:

● Logistics and physical distribution
● Complaints handling
● After-sales service

The activities which customer service shares with other activities include:

● Provision of information to customers before, during and after sale
● Selling/order-taking and invoicing
● Packaging and presentation
● Credit, terms of payment and debt collection

All these activities can be thought of in terms of a customer service sequence, which is described and discussed in the next chapter.

There are one or two common usages, which may be slightly confusing when thinking about customer service as we have defined it.

Customer service and quality

The word 'quality' is sometimes linked to customer service, notably in the Total Quality Management (TQM) philosophy. Clearly this linkage is valid; quality is essential to customer satisfaction. However, quality is as important in the primary activity (or service) as in the secondary, customer-service activities. The quality of the beans in the can is at least as important as the quality of the service at the checkout.

For this reason, quality does not seem to be specially related to customer service, or synonymous with it.

Personal service

The phrase 'personal service' is often used, usually with a sigh in the voice and nostalgia in the mind. But satisfactory customer service may be completely non-personal. Consider the following situations:

- Cooking your own supper
- Getting your meal from a coin-operated machine
- Eating at a self-service cafeteria
- Eating in a restaurant with full waiter service
- Having your meal prepared and served to your own personal requirements by professional caterers

This follows a continuum of 'personal service', from zero to total. But service is provided in each case (except the first) and each may be exactly what is required by a particular customer.

The same comments could be made about farms which offer a 'pick your own' facility, supermarkets with ready-packed fruit, the specialist greengrocer and the van that delivers to our door. Even the pick your own farmer offers service which clearly meets a customer need and may be well or badly provided.

Customer or consumer?

The words 'customer' and 'consumer' may be used of the same individual, but suggest a difference of emphasis. As has been said, 'customer' may describe a person or organisation throughout a transaction; 'consumer' seems appropriate to that person or organisation only in the phase when they have bought and are using the product or service.

Consumers have raised a high profile in recent years, culminating in the consumerist movement, and the legislation and protective agencies this has generated. This has been one, but only one factor in the steadily growing emphasis on customer service.

Organisations that give customer service

Many organisations, naturally including much of the retail sector, have always seen themselves as customer-driven. Some household names in this area such as Marks and Spencer and Sainsbury have led the way in customer service.

The industrial sector presents a profoundly mixed picture, with product- and profit-driven organisations probably heavily outnumbering those that are customer-driven.

Many parts of the commercial sector, including banks and other financial institutions, have recently accepted a customer-driven role. In consequence, they have entered, and are still experiencing, a period of dramatic change that provides a powerful illustration of the effects of this approach. Building societies have led the way, and many banks have also made massive changes, although many of their customers remain unsatisfied.

Surprisingly, some organisations in the 'service' sector have seemed reluctant to adopt a customer-driven approach, despite the nature of their primary product. The most notable has been, perhaps, the passenger transport industry; railways, buses, airlines and air terminals, ferry services and ports. In recent years, however, the customer-driven philosophy has been enthusiastically embraced by some organisations such as British Airways and British Rail. Travel agents mostly appear to realise the need to be customer-driven, while the vast majority of house agents seem to most people to have no understanding whatever of the concept.

Leisure industries such as theatres, cinemas, concert halls, libraries, health and sports centres, public parks, recreation grounds and sports grounds of all kinds vary widely in their approach, but most seem to be product- rather than customer-driven. Catering and hospitality, which many would think of as being in the heart of customer service, present a very mixed picture. Some organisations have taken a strong lead, while others remain apparently uninterested and provide abysmal service.

Some agencies within the public health sector have done much to refocus their thinking towards the customer, but change seems slow and patchy, leaving major aspects and areas untouched. The quality of nursing care is one of the few areas of face-to-face service in which objective measurement has been seriously attempted, using a specially designed instrument known as 'Monitor'.

Education is also a field in which the customer-driven approach seems only partly accepted, although a few changes are apparent in this highly political area.

Citizens' and users' charters are a clear attempt at government level to embed the concept of customer service in legislation. The extent to which the approach will produce real improvements will only become clear in the course of time.

Change is still, in many customers' eyes, overdue in the traditional professions. Some accountants, solicitors, barristers and others have always accepted the customer-driven philosophy; others appear to resist it, in some cases actively. The same may be true of some professional institutions and societies.

Public utilities such as water, electricity, telephone, postal and gas undertakings have also seemed in many cases to resist a customer-driven approach. But here also change is now occurring, and some organisations within the sector are starting to re-appraise their philosophy. The London Electricity Board, for example, is currently initiating a major customer care programme. In one or two cases, customer service has always been a priority for utilities; Cecil Melling, the first Chairman of the Eastern Electricity Board, appointed on nationalisation in 1948, gives[3] a most comprehensive working definition:

> The customer is always right in demanding what he wants at a fair price and right in expecting that, on request, he will receive skilled advice and help in deciding what he wants; right too, in expecting that his demand will be met correctly and expeditiously and, if that cannot be achieved, right in expecting a convincing and courteous explanation; right in expecting that, should he complain about any defect in goods or service, his complaint will be dealt with promptly and thoroughly by some knowledgeable person who is able and willing to correct whatever defect be disclosed, or, if correction be found unnecessary or impracticable, right in expecting helpful advice and a careful explanation.

Would that, forty-five years later, more utilities embraced similar policies.

Except insofar as they may be covered by 'Charters', local and national government departments, despite the proud title of 'Civil Service' borne by the latter, seem for the most part to have felt unable to embrace a customer-driven approach. This has generally included even those, such as housing departments at local level and such operations at national level as passport offices and the Driver and Vehicle Licensing Centre, which operate in close customer contact. Privatisation and competitive tendering for an increasing range of such services is felt by some to have shown benefits. The full picture will be several years in emerging.

Thought-starters

1. In your own experience, which sectors of the economy (a) most and (b) least fully accept the customer-driven approach? What are the reasons for these differences? Are they changing, and if so, why?
2. Does your organisation give customer service? If so, what departments, jobs and individuals are involved, and in what ways?
3. Do you personally give customer service? If so, in what ways?
4. Would you consider your organisation to be customer-driven? If not, what is its principal drive, and why?
5. What are the links in the supply chain behind what your organisation provides? To what extent do they affect the service you are able to give to your customers?
6. In what ways might your organisation most effectively add value through enhanced customer service to the goods (or services) it already provides?

References

1. Theodore Levitt; *The Marketing Imagination*, The Free Press, 1983.
2. Frances Gaither Tucker; 'Creative Customer Service Management', *International Journal of Physical Distribution*, Vol. 13, No 3, 1983.
3. Cecil J Melling; *Light in the East*, Eastern Electricity, 1987.

2
THE CUSTOMER SERVICE SEQUENCE

THE PHASES OF customer service follow the sequence of any complete business transaction:

1. Market research
2. The pre-ordering climate
3. Buying/ordering
4. The period from order to delivery
5. Packaging/presentation
6. Accuracy, completeness and convenience of delivery
7. Complaints handling
8. Debt collection
9. After-sales service and support

The emphasis on each element will vary depending upon the nature of the organisation and the transaction; but each will always be present in one form or another.

We will now look at each phase in turn, highlighting a few examples of their relevance in particular sectors, whether industrial, commercial, service, or public. Customers' expectations, hopes and fears are surprisingly similar in each phase, and we shall also try to identify what these are.

1. Market research

Unless we know what our customers want, what they actually get will be a matter of chance. Establishing their needs and expectations should be the foundation for everything else we do.

Market research is a long-established tool for improving the relevance and appeal of the primary product or service, but it is much less used to investigate the field of customer service. If, however,

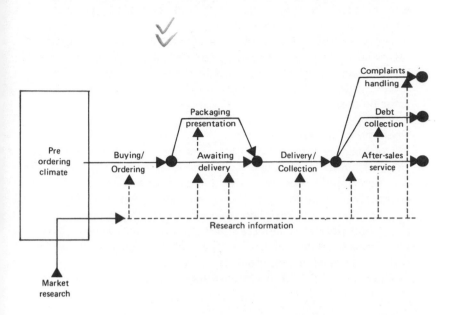

Figure 2. *The customer service sequence*

we accept the vital importance of customer service in achieving growth and success, and the need to become customer-driven in our approach, we shall want to make full use of the tools of market research to learn about our customers' needs for service.

In Chapter 13, an approach to the customer service survey is described. This is put forward as an exercise to provide the initial information about its customer service situation needed by an organisation that has not examined this area previously. It will thus provide a firm base for improvement. Some organisations may conduct such a survey at regular, perhaps annual, intervals. But they may also want to supplement its findings with research into the need for, or consequences of, any major change in the customer service area.

2. The pre-ordering climate

This is the environment surrounding a potential customer before he orders or tries to order. His awareness of product and suppliers may be vague and unfocused. In some cases, he may not know clearly what his own needs are.

The tasks of selling and giving customer service are closely interrelated during this phase. But the potential customer needs information before he gets enmeshed in the selling process. The potential customer needs both product and supplier information.

Product information

Many product (and service) areas are today extremely complex. They also change with enormous speed. Not only the layman, but organisational buyers may easily become out of touch with what is currently available. Suppliers, especially perhaps larger and longer established suppliers, may fall into the trap of assuming that potential customers are familiar with what they have to offer, while potential customers may be failing to buy, or to buy what they really need, out of ignorance.

The customer will have questions such as:

What is on offer that might meet my needs?
What is it called?
What can it do for me, and what will it not do?
What sort of costs are involved?
What is the outline technology, and the basic terms I should know?

The computer industry benefits from a myriad books, magazines and courses offering appreciation to potential customers suffering from various degrees of ignorance. But few other sectors are. There may be scope for individual manufacturers or trade associations to produce or stimulate production of similar laymen's guides, especially in areas in which technological change is rapid.

There are many service areas in which the great majority of potential customers probably have very little information. These may include sectors such as road and rail passenger services, further education, and public leisure facilities. The impression is strong that in all of these many potential customers fail to buy simply because they do not know what is on offer.

In the private sector, it is possible that some areas may also suffer from a fundamental lack of background information for those who do not already buy. These may include, for example, professional services such as those offered by surveyors or solicitors, and perhaps the services of less widespread organisations such as bespoke tailors and auction houses.

At national government level, provision of information for potential customers about the social security services appears to form an intractable problem, despite attempts by the department involved and the many private agencies working in the field. Perhaps here the failure is with the product. The possible findings of market research into customers' needs and expectations in this area might provide fascinating food for thought.

Supplier information
In regard to suppliers, the customer needs to know such things as:

What sort of organisation supplies the product?
Are there many competitive suppliers, few, or only one?
Do they specialise, or what are the principal differences
    between them?
Do they supply direct to users?
How do I find and contact them?
What initial questions should I ask?
Will the situation involve negotiation or bargaining?
How far can I go without incurring obligation?

The starting point for finding out is often directories, especially telephone and classified telephone directories. But these may not always give what is wanted, or may be difficult to understand.

Indexing in particular may be a problem. Local government services such as schools, colleges, hospitals and leisure facilities appear often to be indexed by organisational hierarchy (owning department of owning authority) in a way which is meaningless to the majority of potential customers. Indexing by the actual name of the institution would be much more helpful.

Some, such as the hospitality and tourism sectors, are particularly richly catered for with supplier information. Other sectors may feel something could be gained by studying and applying their approach.

3. Buying/ordering

This phase of customer service is also one in which selling and giving service are inextricably intertwined. But as in the previous phase, the two cater for different customer needs, both of which must be met. The customer will continue to need knowledge; but because he is now a buyer, he will evaluate that knowledge and may look for adjustment by the supplier in what is offered to him; a relationship is being developed.

Buying information

Apart from knowledge of the primary product, the customer will need information on how it is supplied; quantities available, usual order size and frequency, delivery time and method and packaging.

The organisational buyer is usually in the hands of a salesman during this phase, who should be able to provide all the information needed. But salesmen may sometimes feel under pressure to close the present sale, despite a lack of the information that alone could guarantee long-term satisfaction. The same may be true of the various agents selling insurance and other financial services to the private buyer.

'What width d'you want them?' demanded the assistant in the dry-cleaner's shop, of the man who had brought in his trousers to have the bottoms narrowed. 'I'm not sure,' was the hesitant reply. 'What is the usual width?' 'There's a tape-measure there,' replied the assistant wearily, turning to the next customer.

The retail sector can be surprisingly bad in this phase, as many men attempting to buy meat at a traditional butcher's shop have found out.

Here also rail services may lose out; only a small proportion of potential users can, according to surveys, read timetables; an even smaller proportion may be able to fathom the complexities of the fare structures on offer.

Financial information

The customer needs financial information, including discounts, special offers and quantity price breaks. He also wants to know about terms of payment and credit. The corner shopkeeper selling goods on tick until payday, and the landlord putting drinks on the slate are offering an important customer service. The existence of an appropriate range of methods of payment to meet his circumstances is a vital part of the service any customer will look for from any supplier.

On the other hand, these matters must be approached carefully. Money will always be a delicate area with possibilities of embarrassment, even for the organisational buyer. To talk of deferred payments to a customer about to sign a cheque for the full amount with a feeling of quiet pride may be enough to lose the sale. To misjudge a customer's financial circumstances by offering what are seen as unsuitable terms can give offence, and may lose, if not the current order, the chance of repeat business.

Export

Export markets present special problems in this area.

A study by the Institute of Logistics and Distribution Management[1] has shown that the majority of UK exporters still quote prices for export orders on ex works or FOB terms, thus requiring the customer to pay for and arrange transport through to the ultimate destination. These terms offer a lower level of service than the delivered price usually quoted by local suppliers and exporters from other countries.

The same survey also showed that many UK exporters quoted prices in sterling rather than local currency, with the same negative effect.

Buying procedures

Customers look for the simplest, most friendly buying procedures. They do not relish form-filling, or being asked for apparently unnecessary information. Ordering by telephone, Telex or fax machines may be most convenient for them; computer-to-computer ordering is now practicable in many circumstances. Acceptance of credit card numbers is often of great advantage.

Private individuals suffer more red tape than organisations during this phase.

Having selected my purchases from the shelves, I queue at a till, only to be told that I should 'pay at that till over there'. The would-be employer for whose vacancy I have applied complete with a detailed cv, sends an application form calling for exactly the same information. Life assurance companies, on the other hand, have started to realise how many more policies they will write by reducing to a minimum the complexity of their proposal forms.

4. The period from order to delivery

Customers view this period with misgivings; for some it is at the heart of the customer service problem.

The patient waiting on the benches of the outpatients' department for an invisible consultant, the passenger queueing for the late bus, the works manager desperate for the promised delivery of components, and the client looking day by day for his solicitor's letter feel the same emotions. For satisfaction, they need delivery as promised. They also need and have a right at any time to accurate information on the status of their order and the true cause of any delay.

Over-optimistic delivery promises by an eager sales force can do much harm to customer relationships. The customer usually wants a realistic delivery promise more than he wants speed.

Customers have a particular fear of the few suppliers who may accept orders, even payment, for goods that they cannot deliver within an acceptable lead time. Goods may be so delayed as to incur heavy customer costs or completely lose their utility. The lawnmower ordered in May and finally delivered in October is of precious little value to the customer. Consumer protection bodies are already making their views known on such sharp practice.

The 'just-in-time' or 'kanban' concept depends upon the highest standards in delivery. While not working to such extreme limits of accuracy, many organisations have now reduced their stockholdings and rely on delivery within a specified period.

5. Packaging/presentation

Customers look for their goods (and service) to be packaged and presented conveniently. Attractive packaging before purchase is an aid to selling; after purchase, packaging becomes an aspect of service.

The customer needs packaging that is suitable for carriage and storage, that is easy to remove (or to leave in place during use), and that can be disposed of easily or, as a bonus, has a secondary use.

Biscuits in plastic packs that can hardly be entered without crushing the contents; sweetener tablets in containers whose hole allows a stream to escape at once; plastic toothpaste tubes that will not roll up; frozen food in glossy, highly-coloured packs that effectively hide their contents; milk in cartons that will neither open nor pour: these are some of the service problems packaging presents to the customer.

inconvenient to the customer, but to the rest of the general public for centuries to come.

6. Accuracy, completeness and convenience of delivery

The customer expects the quality, quantity and specification of his goods or service to be as ordered. He also expects the time and place of collection or delivery to be convenient. Convenience of time will include such things as opening hours (his and the supplier's) and the relationship to public holidays and weekends.

The customer will be anxious about the possibility of damage, and will not want split deliveries unless previously agreed.

Off-loading may present problems of demarcation. Unhelpful or wrongly briefed drivers can cause problems for customers without suitable handling equipment or the requisite brute strength.

7. Complaints handling

Customers want complaints to be heard positively and understandingly, to be reported by a simple and friendly procedure, to be investigated (if investigation is needed) thoroughly, to be resolved with the utmost speed, and to be met with fair and appropriate action.

The ideal outcome for a customer complaining about goods is to have the choice of immediate refund or replacement. Some large retail chains have set the highest standards in this phase.

The various statutory bodies set up to protect customers with complaints against public monopolies probably achieve little. Their lack of powers and bureaucratic procedures effectively discourage their use in the majority of cases. Similar feelings are often expressed against some trade associations and similar bodies that appear to offer customer protection but in practice do not.

8. Debt collection

Customers do not wish to be dunned unnecessarily, exploited by an overweening supplier, or to suffer from accounting errors. Worst of all, they fear damage to their credit status through secret and incorrect reports and references.

They do not like large or monopoly suppliers who use their market strength to make life difficult for customers by insisting on early or even prepayment.

The powers of those public services that can simply pull a plug or throw a switch on their debtors (or apparent debtors) give rise to much anxiety among customers.

9. After-sales service and support

'Service' refers to routine servicing, whether by contract or on demand, to repairs, and to the supply of spare parts. 'Support' refers to the availability of consumables, user advice and training.

The area of after-sales service is a microcosm of the other phases of customer service, from pre-ordering climate through to debt collection. As such, it suffers the same problems but with one vital addition. Because it is 'after sales', the customer is tied to the product, and therefore feels, rightly, that the supplier has a moral obligation to him. Customers who are so tied will have greater expectations than while their options were still open.

Customers require availability of service, spares, consumables and advice with sensible pricing and good workmanship.

Service facilities may be too few, too hard for customers to find or use conveniently, staffed by badly trained personnel, or with inefficient documentation.

This is another phase in which freely available information is essential to the customer. Instruction brochures and manuals are frequently grossly inadequate, apparently put together, if at all, as a hurried afterthought. Some customers' problems are caused by misuse of the product they have bought, or failure to use it to best advantage, and the support needed after a sale includes the ready and continuing availability of advice. The computer software industry remains abysmal in this respect. The manuals issued with some of the leading products frequently parade the endless ingenuity of their makers while totally ignoring the simplest needs of their users. If car manuals were similarly produced, few drivers would learn how to turn the ignition on, let alone drive off.

Customers expect that any consumables needed to use their equipment will be readily available.

The supply of spares, particularly for ageing equipment, is a major and never-ending source of customer anxiety. Customers feel in danger of exploitation from suppliers who charge excessively for spare parts and service, or who try to insist on unsuitable service contracts. The increasing number of expensive 'service contracts' has become a further area of exploitation by some suppliers.

Some organisations deliberately refuse to supply spares to customers. The pretext given is either that customer servicing might (as with some electrical apparatus) be dangerous, or that it would breach the conditions of the guarantee. Most customers would prefer to have the option to service their own property.

Customers fear that the standard of service workmanship may bear little relationship to the quality of the original product. In the worst cases, as with some garages, 'servicing' is seen as simply an open cheque for work not done.

Thought-starters

1. List any serious problems you have personally experienced in the various phases of the customer service sequence (a) at work, and (b) in private life.

   Which phase has, in your experience, given rise to the most serious and frequent failures? Why do you think this is?
2. Has your organisation included aspects of customer service in any market research it has undertaken? If so, which aspects were they, and what was established? If not, how do you know what service your customers need?
3. Which phases of the customer service provided by your own organisation cause most concern? What goes wrong, why, and what might be done to improve it?

Action points

1. Incorporate customer service aspects into all future market research (page 33).
2. Produce or stimulate production of laymen's guides to your area of business (page 34).
3. Check directory entries including indexing, and place additional entries if necessary (page 35).
4. Ensure that a full range of financial options is available and known to customers (page 36).

5. Check export terms of trade and revise, if necessary, to 'delivered' in local currency (page 37).
6. Ensure ordering procedures are the simplest possible, using telephone, credit cards, or computer-to-computer as appropriate (page 37).
7. Introduce disciplines within the sales area to ensure unrealistic delivery promises are not made (page 38).
8. Improve service aspects of packaging (page 38).
9. Brief delivery drivers to help with handling when necessary (page 39).

Reference

1. *UK Export Terms of Trade—A Survey*, Institute of Physical Distribution Management, 1985.

PART 2

PERSON-TO-PERSON

3
FACE-TO-FACE:
Why it Goes Wrong

DIRECT CONTACT BETWEEN people is the heart of customer service. Whether they are buying and selling peanuts or atomic power stations, people like to deal with people. Whatever the business, and whatever the organisation, it is ultimately the person-to-person relationships between supplier and customer that will make or break it. Catalogues, letters, telephones and the other modes of communication will help, but the parties will always need, in the end, to deal face to face.

Face-to-face contact offers the best way of exchanging information, of weighing up the other party, of negotiating, of solving problems, and of establishing long-term relationships.

If face-to-face contact goes wrong, even the best product has a poor chance of producing customer satisfaction; if face-to-face contacts are good, even a mediocre product will be seen in the best light.

Real and long-lasting improvement in face-to-face customer service cannot be achieved in isolation; an exercise in this field alone is simply treating symptoms. Success can only come from learning the needs of our customers, from examining our current performance, and from looking at each element that contributes to that performance; organisation structure, systems, hardware, equipment and communications of all kinds. To try to improve face-to-face skills alone may produce short-term changes; deep, long-lasting benefit can only come from ensuring that every element in our customer service activity supports and reinforces the efforts of our customer-contact staff; we must become customer-driven.

In this chapter we will examine the reasons why, despite the fact that we are all in our turn customers, contacts may go wrong. The following chapter will suggest some action points for management improvement and list straightforward do's and don'ts of effective customer contact. Finally, in Chapter 5, we will look at apparently difficult customer behaviour, and offer some pointers for dealing with the awkward customer.

Most of us experience similar feelings when we are in the role of customer; why, when we are in the role of supplier, does face-to-face service sometimes go wrong? There are many causes, some the result of deep-seated social attitudes, some caused by management failure (see Figure 3 below).

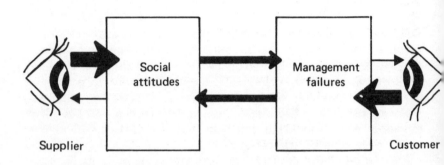

Figure 3. *Customer contact: why it goes wrong*

Social attitudes

The first category includes particularly sensitive aspects of present-day society. We will need to fasten our safety belts and prepare for a bumpy ride. The journey may be depressing, but it is essential to bring such causes into the light of day so that we can have a chance of improving the situation, or at least of avoiding the harm that these factors may do to our customer relations.

The political aspect

To work as a waiter, receptionist, behind a counter, on a switchboard, or in any other role which involves taking the orders of another may suggest the relationship of master and servant—even master and slave. For some, these feelings may be generalised and acquire a bitterly political dimension. People who take this view may see both the giving and receiving of service as immoral acts, which strike at the concept of equality.

This book would not presume to challenge the political beliefs of its readers. But it does seem legitimate and helpful to raise the questions: do political attitudes affect the face-to-face service we and our colleagues are prepared to give, and if so, is there anything we could or should try to do about it?

Related to this aspect is the matter of giving gratuities for some types of service. This also is a very thorny field, but one every organisation providing service needs to enter and explore thoroughly. The attitudes bred by gratuities may work against the concept of good service in every area.

The racist aspect

Here again, we must venture on to difficult ground.

The memory of the days of colonialism, when dominant Anglo-Saxons were served by those with other languages and other coloured skins, still lies in the subconscious. Sadly, it has been reinforced by the extensive employment of immigrants to Britain in service industries such as public transport.

This evil and unpleasant cross-current harms, among so many other things, the concept of good service as a duty all providers owe to all customers, irrespective of race, colour or creed.

The sexist aspect

This is also important, and cannot be dismissed lightly. The belief affects both parties in face-to-face service. It suggests that men neither wish to give nor receive customer service, and that it is women who want it and are best at giving it.

'Whoever heard of this nonsense of service?' runs the argument as applied to the customer. 'In a cowpunchers' speakeasy, or the canteen of a North Sea oil rig? What would be the result of trying this pansy acting in the bothy in a scrap metal yard, or a transport caff? Give men the goods they have paid for, without frills, and that's that.'

It is women, the argument suggests, who are anxious in business situations. They are more sensitive, more aware of interpersonal tensions, less direct in approach, more in need of help and guidance, less likely to be experienced and skilful in the wicked ways of the business world. They expect manners, especially from men, dislike strong language, and are easily offended, particularly by a failure to treat them with respect.

This argument seems fairly easy to dispose of as it is applied to the customer. There can be no doubt that the kind of service wanted in a transport caff or the canteen of an oil rig is different from that needed in a tea-room in a south coast town. To give what his customers see as good service, the supplier must find out his customers' expectations and wants. The fewer preconceptions or stereotypes he has, the more effectively he will be able to do this. The differences may, or may not be related to sex, tradition, income or other factors; the supplier will do well not to waste time and effort looking at causes, which are in any case likely to be far more complex than they appear, but concentrate on effects.

As applied to the supplier, the argument claims that men are inevitably uncomfortable giving customer service. Every aspect worries them, and they do it only under pressure and protest. Smiling, being nice to strangers and feeding their fads is women's work.

Meanwhile, the argument continues, women fit into the service scene perfectly. The mothering instinct ideally fits them to soothe, smooth and help others. They enjoy it, and do it naturally.

Is this a real, or a purely sexist argument?

This side of the question is of great practical importance; some years ago a UK airline refused to employ male stewards until brought before the Equal Opportunities Commission. While most employers observe the provisions of the Equal Opportunities Act, it remains a fact that the vast majority of customer-contact jobs in all sectors are filled by women.

The whole armoury of anti-sexist arguments seem valid here. Without rehearsing them at length, they may be summarised by saying that the individual variations of behaviour, attitudes and skills in the customer/supplier situation are so wide as to swamp completely any purely sexual distinctions that may exist. We have all met waiters, doctors, teachers, salesmen or holders of any other service role who display the highest interpersonal skills irrespective of sex. Concern and a desire to help are not the exclusive female preserve tradition suggests, any more than tough directness and effective negotiating skills belong only to males.

The exploitation of weaker groups

It is a sad fact that organisations of all types, large and small, public and private, tend to oppress those they feel are in weaker competitive positions or small minorities.

If you are particularly tall or stout, you will find problems in buying clothes. If you are disabled, you will find problems getting into vehicles and buildings. If you find writing difficult, you face problems in getting many of the rights to which you are fully entitled. National Servicemen during the 1950s noticed the difference in the face-to-face service they received when in uniform compared with their treatment when they were in mufti.

The treatment often meted out to children, especially boys, provides another illustration. A cinema confiscates cans of soft drink from its youthful patrons as they enter, claiming they are 'not allowed inside', and refuses to return them. A bus inspector, finding a boy who has mislaid his school bus pass, orders him to get off and walk, despite the rain and the three miles to go through darkened London streets. Some park-keepers may pass the time by telling young boys to stop doing whatever they are currently enjoying. Even police, it is claimed, may stop, question and detain youths whose only apparent offence is to be young.

Those who do these things probably believe that they will not harm relationships with the larger and more articulate body of their customers. There are many reasons for being sure that judgement is, in the long term, wrong. Little boys, like little girls, get bigger every day.

The problem of size

The smaller the organisation, the less likely the needs of face-to-face service are to get forgotten.

If Mrs Jones flounces out of the corner shop offended, and proceeds (as she surely will) to tell all her friends what was said to her, it is likely that the effect on sales will be noticed within days. If our new assistant can't get on with people, we shall soon be told, in no uncertain terms. In such an organisation, the link between cause and effect—between customer service and prosperity—is clear for all to see.

The larger the organisation, the less obvious and direct is this connection. If we have several million customers through a hundred branches each week, the effect of an occasional row at the checkout in Much Binding may remain hidden for a long time.

Monopolies

There are special dangers in being a monopoly, whether in the public or the private sector.

The causal connection between satisfying customers' needs and the prosperity and very existence of such an organisation may have been broken by its marketing strength, or perhaps by a system of subsidies and the obligation to provide services that are uneconomic.

The meter-reading and maintenance services, for example, of most public supplying organisations make no attempt to meet the convenience of the private customer. They will neither make nor keep appointments with householders, who are expected to hold themselves available, despite the demands on their own time.

For many years, telephone customers would be required to share party lines without the option. Perhaps the ultimate was reached by the ruling that when the automatic dialling facility had broken down, customers were required to pay the higher 'operator' rates if they wished to make a call. It is difficult to imagine a more complete negation of customer service than this.

It is instructive to see how changes have been made when a monopoly is broken, or under threat of being broken. Suddenly, just before the competing railway was electrified, and with other carriers entering the market, air passengers who had previously been forced to kick around London or Glasgow airports for an hour or more before their flight were told that a 'Shuttle' had been invented on to which they could walk at once. As possible competition approached, and the option to plug in other suppliers' equipment was made legal, the regulations of the GPO and its successor about telephones underwent a dramatic change. Customers who had previously been told they could have any telephone they wanted provided it was regulation black and fitted by the authority were wooed with an endless variety of colours and models and an open invitation to plug them in.

In a monopoly, the incentive to find out what the customer wants and to provide it is inevitably weak. Those who make the effort may be surprised by the results, and may find, for example, that many customers would be prepared, if necessary, to pay more to receive specific service improvements.

The dangers of a sellers' market

This is perhaps the parallel within the private sector to the public monopoly.

The years of the Second World War, and the following decade of peace, conditioned a whole generation of UK suppliers and customers. Rationing, shortages, uncertain and lengthy deliveries, substitution of inferior products, lack of spares, waiting lists and queues affected every area of the economy. In retail sales and consumer goods, public transport, and throughout the supply chain, the customer learnt he must wait patiently and meekly to get something, and that he must offer thanks if, when he got it, it did what was expected. The chances of its continuing to do this for very long would, of course, be limited by lack of spares and service engineers to fit them.

This attitude has now nearly disappeared, but its effects have gone deep, and it has left scars on many sectors such as, perhaps, the motor and garage industries.

Management failings

The factors making for bad face-to-face service which are the result of management failure include:

Bad morale

'No chance of the fitter coming before next month; this outfit couldn't run an ice factory in Lapland, love.' Unhappy staff will consciously or unconsciously appeal for help by taking it out on the customer. An organisation that suffers from a demotivated workforce will find it very hard to give good customer service. Indeed, this is probably the first area in which the symptoms of falling morale will show.

The quality of face-to-face customer service is very closely related to the overall morale of the organisation. To attempt to improve face-to-face service without solving the deeper problems is to treat symptoms. To run cosmetic 'service' campaigns may make small and temporary improvements, but will otherwise be water poured into the sand.

Bad selection

Front-line customer contact, whether as a supermarket cashier, a systems analyst, a bus conductor, a doctor, a waiter, a teacher, an airline steward, a solicitor or whatever, requires skills that are as specific as for any other aspects of work, and harder to find than many. However, the sources from which and the methods by which we choose staff for such jobs often completely fail to recognise this fact.

In some cases (eg systems analyst), staff for front-line posts may be selected, perhaps as a promotion, on their technical competence. In others (eg commissionaire), they may be filled by long-service personnel who deserve well of their organisation or their country. In others (eg solicitor), they may be appointed after professional training which does not include customer-contact skills. Others (eg doctor's receptionist), will be part-time staff, perhaps housewives or those who have retired from other work. Probably the great bulk of front-line staff (eg shop assistant, garage forecourt attendant), are seen as starting grades, recruited direct from outside the organisation, possibly from unqualified school-leavers or Jobcentres.

It is not suggested that any of these sources is inappropriate; in most circumstances, each may be the only way. However, if first-rate face-to-face customer service is our aim, this does suggest that we must give the actual process of selection and recruitment the most careful attention. We must thoroughly examine our selection criteria, to ensure they include customer-contact skill and interest. We must also consider our selection methods, to ensure they are sufficiently professional and make use of all available techniques for judging, preferably measuring, those skills and aspects of personality which affect the giving of service.

If we leave selection to a busy supervisor, untrained in selection procedures and unsupported by professional help, we can hardly be surprised at mistaken choices or failures in face-to-face service.

Lack of training

Given the problems with the sourcing and selection of staff, the training of front-line customer contact staff must be absolutely vital. Sadly, even the most responsible organisations frequently appoint employees to posts with extensive face-to-face customer contact without giving them training in the necessary customer contact skills.

Methodical training is as necessary as for any other skill: pre-appointment training before undertaking the duties, booster and updating training throughout the period of an appointment; corrective training as need arises, and in-depth training as promotion is gained. This is referred to again at more length in Chapter 14.

Lack of a career structure

Unless it is reasonably possible for those filling front-line customer-contact posts to progress upwards, good calibre staff will not want such posts. If our managers are recruited from outside, perhaps at graduate level, then our shop assistants are unlikely to be of high potential.

On the other hand, organisations that use customer-contact posts as an essential phase in the development of its upwardly mobile staff, will do a great deal to ensure its face-to-face customer service is effective.

Inadequate supervision

Supervisors and managers in departments with extensive face-to-face customer contact should not be appointed unless they have the skills, the experience and the willingness to guide and support their staff through the problems such contact poses.

Customer contact together with other duties

Technical and specialist staff of all kinds frequently hold posts in which customer-contact and technical work are mixed. In consequence, they face the particular danger that they are likely to have been selected on their technical skills, and unlikely to have been selected for or trained in customer-contact skills. For this reason, they may feel exposed and insecure when in contact with customers, and take refuge in the technical nature of their work, consciously or unconsciously ignoring the importance of the customer service element.

A brilliant systems analyst, for example, who upsets all the customers with whom he works is probably more harmful to his organisation than a less skilled analyst who forms first-rate customer relations.

Occasionally, there may even be overt resistance to the needs for customer service. Some skilled specialists may say, perhaps in so many words, 'I am paid, trained and employed to (say) conduct heart transplant operations. I do it very well. Keeping customers happy is something I neither enjoy nor have time for; it is and should be the job of others.' This is a pity, as patients and other customers respond to treatment as whole people rather than just as cases.

Industrial relations problems

Sometimes there may be industrial relations aspects, as when a particular group or grade makes customer contact the basis of demands for enhanced payment. If so, the problem needs to be grasped swiftly, before a long-running and destructive battle ensues in which the chief sufferer is the customer.

Status

Customer-contact staff in junior posts may see 'being nice to the public' as a characteristic of their subordinate position. They may feel the need not to be nice in order to assert their status as an individual. Servility is a bigger threat to someone who may feel he is seen as a servant than to someone who more clearly is not.

If we want our staff to serve customers well, they must know that they and the work they do is respected and appreciated. This is not just a matter of an occasional pat on the head. All the signals the organisation sends them must say the same; genuine consultation and involvement in decisions that affect them, conditions of employment and a working environment that matches those of other key staff. The respect they give customers will reflect the respect we give to them.

Situational conflict

Some jobs have what may be termed 'built-in situational conflict'. These will include posts such as traffic wardens, police, park-keepers, rangers, private security staff, ticket collectors, car park attendants, night-club bouncers and others.

Other posts and organisations may have a lower but latent level of situational conflict. These include any post in which it is necessary to sit behind a grille, to wear a uniform, or to accept or refuse permission of some sort to customers, such as counter staff in banks, building societies, and post offices.

The needs of good customer service in conflict positions will only differ in degree from the needs of other staff: careful selection, good and continuing training and proper management support. The extent to which this help is now given probably varies widely, with consequent effects on the success of customer contact.

Incidental activities

Incidental activities may have an effect on customer relations. These activities may, for example, be digging up a road, driving a heavy goods vehicle, or picketing a place of work. It is impossible to ignore them, even though they are strictly irrelevant. All employees of an organisation inevitably represent that organisation to outsiders, whether they are paid to do so, wish to do so, or not.

The same is true of more remote situations. If customer and member of staff meet in a disco and gossip, fight or fall in love, there will be effects on the organisational contact. If an employee is a local councillor, his views and actions on the council will reflect, willy-nilly, on his employers and colour the view of customers. Life cannot be lived in watertight compartments.

Thought-starters

1. Have you been aware of any of the deep-seated social attitudes listed in the chapter affecting customer service? If so, when and with what result?
2. Do any of these attitudes affect the face-to-face service given by your organisation? If so, which, and how might they be changed?
3. Do any of these attitudes affect your own face-to-face behaviour? If so, which, does it concern you, and what might bring about a change?
4. Do you see differences between the sexes as (a) customers, and (b) suppliers of service? If so, what are they, and are they innate or conditioned? Should they affect the service suppliers give, and if so, how?
5. Do you agree monopolies abuse their power with the customer? If so, how, and what might be done to rectify the situation?
6. Consider any sectors or industries which are or were in a sellers' market. Which were they, and what effect, if any, has it had on their customer service?
7. What do you see as the top three causes of less than perfect face-to-face service in your own organisation, and how could they be eliminated?

Action points

1. Brief staff not to exploit children and other weaker groups of customers (pages 48-9).

2. Upgrade recruitment and selection procedures of front-line staff (pages 51-2).
3. Train all front-line staff in customer-contact skills (page 52).
4. Provide genuine career opportunities for all front-line staff (page 53).
5. Train or deselect technical experts with inadequate customer-contact skills (page 53).

4
FACE-TO-FACE:
Service With a Smile

IF FACE-TO-FACE customer contact is a problem, then the organisation almost certainly has deeper troubles.

Where and what the trouble may be, only study will tell. It may be poor supervision, equipment or working conditions, or any one of a combination of the factors listed in the last chapter. It may even be that the product or service itself is at fault; at the end of the day, good customer service can only be supported by a good product.

Any action to correct major failings in face-to-face customer contact must be based on a thorough examination and rectification of the underlying causes, whatever they may be; only then can the behavioural problems be tackled with any hope of long-term success.

Respecting people

People reflect the respect they themselves receive. If those we live and work with respect us, we respect ourselves; if we respect ourselves, we are likely to respect those we meet and deal with. If, on the other hand, we are denied respect as individuals, we will tend to pass on this negative attitude to others. An organisation which regards its front-line customer-contact staff as the bottom of the heap cannot grumble if they serve its customers badly.

Unfortunately this is exactly the situation in many organisations; as was pointed out in the last chapter, customer-contact staff are often on the very lowest rung of the organisational ladder. In many cases they are recruited from those with few qualifications, receive little or no behavioural training, and have few or no promotional prospects. They may be part-time, possibly temporary staff, and are likely to move on rapidly if there are other jobs to go to.

This is the biggest management challenge in customer contact.

An ideal solution might be to regrade such posts to recognise their importance to the success of the organisation, but for many reasons this will usually be impossible. A second move may be to offer some bonus to such staff to enhance their position and also to act as a stimulus to effective performance. This solution is used in many organisations, and can offer good results. However, any system relying on bonus payments may give rise to problems of performance measurement, abuse and escalation, and must be carefully designed and operated. At best, this solution can apply only in a limited range of circumstances.

Some organisations use devices such as name badges and other techniques which help to emphasise the identity of the individual. These may be useful, although occasionally they may cause more embarrassment than they do good. To be effective, we must go much deeper than this.

It is imperative that we use every technique of good management at our disposal, including particularly those mentioned in the last chapter, such as effective resourcing, selection, training and supervision of staff. Other ways must be found to convey the all-important message that our front-line staff are a key to the success of the whole enterprise, and that their unique contribution as individuals is known and valued.

The systems, equipment and conditions in which such staff work will always reflect to them the esteem in which the organisation holds them. Uniforms or dress will underline, for better or worse, the same lesson.

Best of all is continuously good communication, coupled with real consultation. Motivation is always improved by the belief that we can participate in decisions that affect us, and that our opinion matters to others, especially those with authority. Customer-contact staff who feel that the knowledge and experience they have is valued and will be respected in decisions that affect what they do, will be more likely to respect and serve the organisations' customers well.

There now follows a list of some of the do's and don'ts of customer contact, which are offered as a guide for self-improvement or use in training.

Do's and don'ts of face-to-face contact

The do's include:

Smile

A smile from the start has at least two beneficial effects; it helps to put the customer in a good frame of mind, and it actually helps the smiler to relax and feel good.

It is not, of course, an automatic panacea. A fixed and deadly grin does not achieve a lot, although even this may trigger a natural smile from the customer, which may in turn help us; smiles are infectious.

Look customers in the eye

This gives a feeling of cont..ct, and indeed helps, through eye contact, to establish real communication. In turn, this does a lot to help us judge customer reaction and assess their needs during a transaction.

Some people, however, do not like over-emphasised eye-contact, which may be felt as challenging or intrusive. We should be sensitive to the response we receive.

Weigh the customer up, but keep checking

'You elocutionist speakers are all the same,' said the East End baker good-naturedly, in immediate response to the incoming customer's 'Good-morning'. Digging under a pile of sliced white loaves, he came up triumphantly with an uncut wholemeal. 'That what you was after?' he asked. Of course, he was right.

Customers, like people, inevitably come in types. With experience, we can assess most customers and their needs as soon as they come into view; after all, we are playing them on our home ground. Their dress, where and how they stand, what they do or look at and other hints build up an almost instantaneous picture which can be of great help in helping them.

However, this instant assessment also has dangers. Even the most experienced customer-contact person makes mistakes. We must always be alert to the possibility of error, and leave our options open.

In particular, there is a danger of typing a customer as 'awkward' wrongly, and by treating them in this way we force them to become awkward. This may cause some of the biggest face-to-face customer service problems, and is explored in detail in Chapter 5.

Timing

When to start a conversation with a customer or prospective customer matters a great deal.

Most customers will accept what they judge to be a reasonable cause of delay if they can see some other customer being dealt with or some necessary task being performed. This is why customers become more frustrated in delayed trains than in delayed buses; in the bus, they can usually see what has happened, in the train they can't and need to be told. But we all, as customers, make sharp judgements about unnecessary delay. Chit-chat with a colleague is always unacceptable, and paperwork is suspect. If we disappear, however valid the reason, we may return to find the customer has disappeared as well.

Starting too soon is also wrong; customers do not like to be pounced on before they have got the feel of the place and had time to draw breath.

Few things are worse than dealing with customers out of turn. This may happen by simple oversight, but is more likely to be the result of recognising a regular customer or a friend, or being visually attracted or repelled by a customer. Some customers can be very subtle at attracting attention and jumping the queue. When in doubt, the simple question, 'Who's next, please?' is always acceptable.

The right opening

The first words spoken set the tone of the whole transaction.

Finding the right words can be difficult. 'Can I help you?' may be right; but is grossly over-used, and some people find it offensive. 'May I help?' is preferred by some. There are many other choices. If the prospective customer has already shown interest in something, a question or remark about that is a natural opening.

The right voice

The tone, speed and loudness of the voice may convey aggression, timidity or uncertainty, insolence, boredom or other unhelpful attitudes. We can get nowhere if we cannot be heard clearly; it is off-putting for a customer to have to ask us to repeat what we have said, and many won't bother. On the other hand, shouting appears aggressive.

Listen and appear to listen

The customer wants to be listened to, not just heard. Many customer contacts go sour because what the customer is saying, or trying to say, is misunderstood. Listening is a skill in its own right, at least as difficult as speaking.

But effective listening is not enough. Like justice, listening must not only be done, but be seen to be done. Active listening includes facial expression, encouraging and appropriate noises, some patience, and a general ability not to interrupt. This will not only please the customer, but actually improve the way he communicates with us; not feeling under pressure, he will express himself better. It usually also saves time in the end by helping us to grasp what is wanted accurately and straight away.

Watch the chit-chat

Passing the time of day and exchanging friendly quips and witticisms is now part of giving good customer service. Customers in organisations of all sorts wish to feel a friendly warmth in the contact with someone who is serving them. Gone are the days when waiters at the best restaurants were expected to serve in silence, speaking briefly only when spoken to.

There are traps, however, some of them nasty. The most obvious is to chat too much, thus delaying other customers. We may misjudge individuals, chatting happily to someone who needs to catch a train or who has just lost their wife in a car accident. We may go too far with someone who can't take it; what is a pleasant joke with Mr Brown may be seen as insolence by Mr Green. Finally, we may misjudge our skill as conversationalists or humorists; if we crack jokes with customers it is best if they are good ones.

Offer information and help

'That's nothing to do with you,' replied the railway guard on a crowded train to a passenger who saw what proved to be a private saloon being attached. The response started an argument which nearly ended in blows. The passenger rarely travels by train now.

Many customers are not sure what is available. They need information, by being shown what is available, by being offered literature, or by talking with someone who knows—ourselves, or someone even more knowledgeable.

But they shouldn't be given mental indigestion; too much information is as bad as too little. They should be supplied it as they need it; step-by-step. Sometimes this calls for more than one meeting.

Question tactfully
Some customers are not sure what they want or need. Good customer service suggests that they should be offered help in making up their minds, which will require asking questions. Some customers resent this as an intrusion; others welcome it. The ground must be tested carefully as we go along.

Read the body language
We all talk with our bodies at least as much as with our mouths. Reading this extra language accurately is an enormous help. If the body language and the spoken language appear to contradict each other, we should believe the body language. A customer, for example, who talks as if he were considering a purchase but fidgets and glances at his watch is unlikely to buy.

There is no special magic in it; we all read body language instinctively up to a point. But as with written language, some read it more accurately than others, and it is possible to improve our reading skill substantially.

The most potent organ of body language is the face, and especially the eyes. By keeping good eye contact with the customer we can check whether the expressions of the face and eyes reinforce what is being said (or not said). The face will show interest or boredom, belief or incredulity, liking or distaste far more clearly than the words used.

The stance of the whole body will help to show whether the customer is relaxed or tense, impatient or engaged, wanting to move off or content to stay.

For those who want to learn more about this subject, several books and courses are available.

Use names
We will often learn a customer's name during a meeting, sometimes incidentally (eg from a credit card, passbook or cheque). It is impressive and makes for good relationships to use this knowledge during, and particularly at the end of, the meeting.

End neatly
The end of a conversation is important. It has the best chance of

remaining in the customer's mind after other features of the conversation are forgotten. It may also give an opening for renewing the contact later.

Timing is important. It is easy and dangerous to go on too long. In sales conversations, it is possible to unsell by continuing to talk after the critical moment. Whatever the nature of the contact, we must spot the best moment to conclude.

Some customers do not know how to end a conversation, especially if they have not bought. Indeed, some will actually buy because it seems the only way to end. We should never allow this to happen; such customers will probably be unhappy with what they have bought, and are unlikely to buy again. An alternative conclusion—an easy get-out—may be a much wiser strategy for the long term.

Business cards may be exchanged as a sign that the conversation is ending (if this was not done at the start). This also gives the means to renew the contact at a later date. If business cards are not appropriate, a final piece of literature such as a catalogue or price list may be used in the same way.

Another technique is to make or accept an interruption; to notice another customer, or refer to some other task that you must complete, and observe the reaction. If the customer is ready to go, he will usually take the hint.

If we know the customer's name, we should always use it in saying goodbye.

The don'ts include:

Avoid emotional response
Emotion can be generated in many ways; the 'awkward customer', or the one who appears awkward being the most likely. This is discussed in detail in the next chapter.

Now and then, especially if the customer is of the opposite sex, positive emotional response may endanger effective customer contact. We must maintain professional detachment at all costs.

Don't crowd the customer
'Good service should never embarrass.' Katherine Whitehorn in the *Observer* wrote of the overcrowded customer who 'didn't rush out on the family this morning just to have to interrelate to a lot of strange bank tellers'. Over-insistence on closeness

of relationship is a danger, and we need to weigh up customers' attitudes with care.

Customers, especially the less extrovert kind, may need breathing space during a transaction. They may want to look around further, to consult with a friend or partner, to walk around and come back or simply to stand and think. We need to spot this situation and back off, pleasantly and with some suitable excuse.

Don't carry on other conversations

The ill-mannered habit of carrying on a conversation with another person, whether a colleague or another customer, is impossible to reconcile with good customer service. The present customer must have our full attention.

If we are interrupted, we need to assess how urgent and how lengthy the interruption is likely to be. If very brief, the best tactic is to deal with it immediately and return to our customer with a smile. If it appears to be more lengthy but urgent, we should apologise to the customer with an adequate explanation and deal with the interruption. If it appears to be more lengthy and less urgent, we should apologise to the interrupter and continue the conversation with the customer.

One of the worst mistakes is to allow interruption by a more favoured customer; a regular, an old friend, etc. If this happens, any customer worth his salt will walk away.

Don't try to pull rank

A middle-ranking manager who suffered from a rare and potentially serious medical condition was once sent by his employer for a consultation with the holder of one of the most prestigious medical positions in the country. He approached the single brass plate on the Harley Street residence with doubt, and pressed the bell with trepidation. The door was opened, not by some arrogant flunkey, but by a warm and friendly lady. After barely enough time to get his breath in the homely waiting room, the door was opened by the Great Man, smiling and offering a welcoming hand. During the consultation, notes were taken not by an amanuensis, but by the doctor himself in spidery longhand laid openly on the desk. At the end of the consultation, he offered to explain the situation to the man's fiancée, something he subsequently did clearly and kindly.

The patient could not but contrast his welcome with one he had suffered a few weeks earlier from his local young GP and the dominant lady who performed the role of receptionist for his practice.

One of the most common ways of pulling rank (sometimes quite unconscious) is to refuse to acknowledge a customer, and continue to do what we are doing, be it another task or a conversation with a colleague.

Don't use slang greetings

'Yes, my friend', 'OK, sunshine', 'dear', 'duck', 'love', 'mate', 'kids', nowadays in many situations 'sir' (which is increasingly the prerogative of traffic police, and sounds more insulting as the years go by); if we know someone well, a slang greeting is natural. But the same greeting to a stranger or near stranger may seem anything from unprofessional to downright offensive.

Don't order customers about

A would-be customer entered a crowded shop just before Christmas. Seeing most people circulating towards the left, he decided to move into the less peopled area to the right. Hardly had he started to examine some goods in a case when a stentorian voice boomed down the shop, 'Will you kindly circulate to the left.' The would-be customer walked out at once, blushing violently. Needless to say he has neither used nor recommended that shop since.

Customers do not come to suppliers to be told what they must do. A word which should never be used in customer contact is 'must'. Sometimes the customer may need polite guidance, but short of criminal behaviour he can need nothing more.

Don't blame colleagues or the organisation

Just as in private life it is instant death to criticise someone's wife or husband to their partner, so in business contacts it is death to criticise a colleague to a customer. Every employee *is*, to every customer, the organisation. We can be certain that any criticism of or disloyalty towards our boss, our colleagues or our organisation will be picked up, magnified, and passed gleefully back to whoever it referred to.

Don't show favouritism

To pick a customer out for special favour, or choose them out of

Don't promise what you can't perform
Promises are one way of getting rid of an insistent customer; but a broken promise will return to haunt for far, far longer.

Thought-starters

1. What deeper problems do you feel lie behind any behavioural difficulties in your organisation? How might these be tackled?
2. What place on the organisational ladder do the majority of your customer-contact staff occupy?
3. From what sources are your customer-contact staff recruited? What methods are used for selection? Do they work well, and how might they be improved?
4. Do your customer-contact staff receive behavioural training, and if so at what phases of their job? Is it adequate, and how might it be improved?
5. Are the systems, equipment, working and conditions of your customer-contact staff right for what they must do? If not, how could they be improved?
6. Does your organisation take positive steps to demonstrate its respect for its front-line customer-contact staff, and if so, what?
7. Which of the do's and don'ts of face-to-face customer contact do you feel are most often neglected? Which additional points would you include on the list?
8. Which do's and don'ts do you most often neglect yourself, and why? What do you propose to do about it?

Action points

1. Consider bonus schemes for front-line staff (page 58).
2. Involve front-line staff in making all decisions that affect them (page 58).
3. Upgrade your own customer-contact skills and those of your staff (pages 59-65).

5
FACE-TO-FACE:
The Awkward Customer

A LONDON TRANSPORT ticket collector, quietly doing his duty on late turn one night, challenged a youth trying to pass the barrier without a ticket. For his pains, he was stabbed to death.

Not all customers are angels, any more than all suppliers; we must be realistic.

There are parts of the country where public transport staff on buses and trains work in permanent fear of violence. Their customers may come to them (or at them) in aggressive gangs, sneering and sarcastic, drunk or drugged. Publicans may experience the same problems; today no one in regular public contact can feel fully secure from attacks that may be merely verbal or actually physical.

Nothing we do to make our organisation more customer-centred can detract from our duty to ensure the safety of our staff. If social conditions are such that staff are at risk, then proper precautions must be taken, even at the expense of relations with the majority of reasonable customers. But occasionally panic decisions are made on the basis of a single incident; we should always weigh the evidence as carefully and calmly as possible.

Dishonest customers

There are customers who use the opportunities presented by good, willing service to exploit an organisation or its employees, to cheat, or perhaps to defraud it.

If we allow easy access to the goods, there are some who will shoplift. If we allow credit, there are some who will not pay.

Reasonable customers accept reasonable precautions and what is felt to be reasonable changes with time. Surveillance by closed

67

circuit television is now generally accepted in most situations, although a decade ago many people saw it as a serious intrusion into privacy. But there is always a balance to be struck, and occasional loss may be an acceptable price for easy relations with a vast majority of customers.

We get the customers we deserve

It is said that when police drivers are being trained, they are told that if they are ever involved in any accident, they should regard it as their fault. Perhaps this has a lesson for customer relations.

A restaurant that found its customers were more downmarket than it intended would do no good by complaining. It would either have to change its menus, decor and prices or accept that it must set its sights lower. The initiative in all customer contact originates with the organisation. The organisation is set up to service a certain type of customer in a certain way; if it fails to do this, its marketing is in error. It has the options of rethinking its marketing strategy or accepting and adjusting to the customers it has attracted.

In the long term, an organisation and individuals within an organisation are likely to get the customers they deserve. If our customers are awkward and difficult to deal with; if they present continual problems and make continual complaints, we would do well to search first for the cause within ourselves.

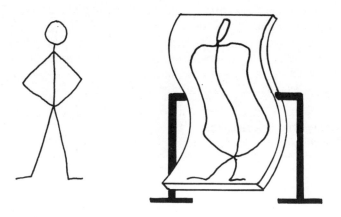

Figure 4. *The awkward customer*

The seemingly awkward customer

'Awkward' customers are not always awkward. A better diagnosis might show that something simple and reparable had gone wrong with the relationship. Examples of this include:

Fear

Fear of several kinds, felt either by the customer or the supplier, lies behind some interpersonal problems. Fear of being exploited by over-demanding customers can produce a defensive, unhelpful approach by staff. In turn, this may generate confrontation and aggressiveness on the part of a customer who feels he is being kept at arm's length, even denied his proper rights and status.

Customers may be in a state of anxiety bordering on fear. Travellers, for example, are often tense and suffering strain. Customers facing what may appear quite ordinary situations may be under a severe strain which the supplier, who is on home ground, may fail to understand. And just as shyness is often mistaken for arrogance, so fear is often mistaken for lack of co-operation.

Disability

Customers, like the rest of us, may suffer from a wide range of disabilities, and may prefer not to make them more obvious than they have to.

In particular, deafness, especially slight deafness, is rarely immediately apparent but can give an impression of deliberate awkwardness. Most of us are hesitant and unsure when faced with mental disability of any kind; to serve all our customers well we will need to develop sensitivity to recognise and skill to help those who suffer in this way.

Physical disability also is not always recognisable at once, and many who suffer it prefer that it should not be. Here also, experience will give us the best chance of serving all customers in the way they want and need.

The same remarks may be made about recognising and helping customers who may be unwell.

Give a dog a bad name

Almost any behaviour can be interpreted favourably or unfavourably, according to how we see it. The same remark, if heard by a friend, may be heard as a clever and harmless witticism; if heard by an enemy it may be interpreted as a sarcastic attempt to set him down.

People tend to live up to what is expected of them. At school, if a teacher expects a pupil to produce bad work, there is a far greater chance that the pupil will actually work badly. The same may happen between ourselves and our customers.

Most of us have many sides to our personality; we behave differently in the company of our partners, our mothers, our business colleagues, the other members of the rugger club, our sworn enemies or those who respect us. In many ways, we truly are different personalities.

If we see the customer as an intrusion, rather than the reason for our organisation's existence, the customer is likely to turn into an intrusion. If we expect the customer to be a nuisance, then the customer may often respond by becoming one. If, however, we welcome the customer and the opportunity to be of service to him, then most customers will oblige by being friendly and helpful in turn.

Miscasting

The scruffily dressed man at the wheel of the Rolls-Royce is in great danger of being arrested for its theft; the tentative and hesitant enquirer may easily be identified as a beginner rather than as the internationally known expert he is. Clothes, accent, manner and the rest may sometimes lead us badly astray.

All customer-contact staff use their skills and experience to typecast customers almost instantaneously. This is not only inevitable; it is an essential and legitimate short cut without which business would take longer and be less effective. But every so often, the process goes wrong.

The worst miscastings involve personal or social biases, possibly based on race, skin colour, or politics. Customer-contact staff who suffer from these should consider whether they would be better in other jobs.

Miscasting may not only occur in face-to-face contact; it is possible to miscast the writer of a letter. Every organisation gets occasional letters from cranks of one sort or another. But judgement may be made on the most superficial factors, such as the quality of the paper, the colour of the ink, the legibility of the writing, spelling, grammar or the address of the writer. Before any letter is identified as crankish, it should be read carefully several times, preferably by at least two people.

Hate at first sight

This is a rare condition but its existence should not be ignored. Just as, every once in a while, people fall instantly and uncontrollably in love, so people may find themselves having to deal with someone for whom they experience a deep, spontaneous and irrational hatred.

This may arise from the dress, accent or appearance of a customer (or of the person serving); more frequently it results from a mutual inability to communicate. Lovers often communicate, even over vast distances, without words; haters usually fail to communicate eyeball to eyeball. Just occasionally, this situation may arise because the two communicate too effectively; their spontaneous insight into each other's character and motivation may render a normal relationship impossible.

The best hope is to recognise this condition as soon as it happens. There is little point in trying to fight it; the hatred will surface sooner or later, and even if it does not, there is little chance that the transaction will come to fruition. If possible, an excuse should be found for passing the contact (*without* unfavourable comment) to a colleague. If not, it may be practicable to postpone business or to complete it by correspondence. If none of these is possible, we must take the deepest of breaths and step forward prayerfully.

The truly awkward customer

When all is said and done, there will always remain a small number of truly awkward customers.

Identifying customers in this way should be postponed for as long as possible; they should be given the benefit of every doubt. What sounds like gratuitous rudeness should be interpreted as a joke gone wrong. Bad language should meet a deaf ear. Lack of co-operation should be seen as simple misunderstanding. Customer-contact staff must be reasonably thick-skinned; it is not a job for the delicate and sensitive flower.

Of those we feel constrained to identify as awkward, the cause may for some be temporary and accessible to skilful surgery; for others, sadly, it may be permanent and inoperable.

Temporary awkwardness is probably a bit like Aristotle's temporary insanity. It includes conditions such as:

Apparent stupidity

This may be the result of extraneous noise, which perhaps we have grown used to, or the result of our inability to explain coherently. In either case, the only way forward must be to assume the fault is ours, and to try again with a friendly and self-deprecating smile.

Apparent stupidity may sometimes be a symptom of the highest intelligence and knowledge. It may appear because the customer knows a lot more than we do, and realises what tripe we are talking, but is too polite, or simply can't be bothered to point it out. We need to be alert to this possibility; we shall not give service if we miss it, and may learn a great deal and make a good friend if we spot it.

Apparent stupidity may, of course, be real stupidity. In this case it should be the object of our best care and help.

Pre-existing anger or irritability

Anger at the very start of a contact may have originated from causes quite outside our control or his; in the absence of evidence, we should not automatically flatter ourselves we are the cause.

Sometimes we may be able to relieve the anger by bringing it into the open. If we know the customer, a lift of the eyebrow or a quizzical look may be sufficient. A touch of humour may work wonders. If we can guess at the cause, we may allude tactfully to it.

If none of these work, the best course is usually to pretend we haven't noticed.

Impatience

Customers who have been kept waiting unduly (even though we were genuinely busy) or who have been passed over may have reason for impatience. Volunteering an apology or explanation usually defuses the anger.

Another cause of impatience may be that the customer is in a hurry. He may have a plane to catch, or his dinner may be waiting on the table. Quick and efficient service will work wonders.

Permanent customer awkwardness includes:

Dishonesty

This worst of awkwardnesses must always be borne in mind. However, as with the others, we must beware of generating an expected response. Nothing will cause a customer to behave more oddly than to follow him round the store, spying on his every move. Police will also confirm that nothing can look more like guilt than injured and confused innocence.

It is even more important to make no accusation or even hint until one is as certain as it is possible to be. The criminal and civil law are both involved here, as well as our reputation. Organisations in which the risk exists should have clear house rules on what to do in cases of suspected shoplifting or theft, which should be explained regularly to all employees.

Political motivation

This is an oddball awkwardness, and can be troublesome when it occurs. The commonest sufferer is a customer who is bitterly opposed to nationalisation, and feels the need to treat employees of nationalised industry as personal enemies. Opposition to trade unions (or a particular trade union, perhaps currently engaged in a dispute) may produce the same symptoms.

There is no known cure for this condition, but sufferers can be helped to a temporary remission by smiles, impeccable manners and efficient service.

Verbal diarrhoea

This is a particularly annoying form of awkwardness in customers. While smiling through the outpouring for as long as possible, a suitable and watertight excuse must be framed. The opportunity given by a pause for breath (even sufferers from this disease must do this, if only momentarily) must be seized with both hands.

NB. It is considered unfair merely to pass sufferers on to a colleague.

Patronisation

This word is not in the Oxford Dictionary, but should be. It means the act of patronising someone. It is done to those who try to serve customers by those who think they are superior to them—people who, were they not customers, would be called snobs.

The temptation to enter a verbal contest is, in such cases, almost overwhelming, particularly as the disease renders the sufferer unable to appreciate his true situation. Sadly, however, the advice must be to resist this approach. Snobs are still customers, and occasionally they *may* actually know the chairman (something which should not make the slightest difference but usually does).

The best ploy is probably to exploit their weakness by playing them right up market, and selling them the most expensive goods in the place.

Sexual harassment

That this may be no laughing matter was tragically demonstrated by the abduction and presumed murder of a London lady estate agent by a supposed client.

Luckily, the bulk of customer and client contact occurs in public. Under these circumstances such behaviour may be no worse than an irritant which most victims are able to cope with. Now and then, it may even be precipitated by the use of sexual attraction in the selling process.

In all contact, professional detachment is imperative; we are working on our own doorsteps.

The professional moaner

'Methinks the Lady doth protest too much,' said Hamlet observantly. There undoubtedly are customers who complain too much. They are a pain in the neck, and best regarded as a test of fire; something we must go through every now and again to ensure we remain up to specification. Viewed in this light, they can be better than an occasional off-the-job training course.

Some experts talk of the 'squeaky wheel', implying that professional moaners will probably get too much of the oil of attention, even of unmerited compensation. It is, however, salutary to think that for every customer who complains too much there may be a hundred who do not complain enough, and who take whatever is thrown at them lying down.

Also, as the Code of Practice on complaints for Local Government and Water Authorities sagely remarks: 'even complaints without substance may be useful as showing a need to work for better understanding of what (we) are trying to do.'

Divorce

In transport, there used to be a role known as the 'common carrier', which implied the legal obligation to carry whatever (within the broadest of limits) he was offered for whoever asked to wherever he wanted it to go. In practice, the role ceased to exist many decades ago, as carrier after carrier exercised his statutory right not to be a common carrier.

At the end of the day, some customer-contact staff may decide correctly that they are unable to help some customers. The organisation may be wrong; the customer may be too demanding; the relationship may have gone irrevocably adrift. Such events must be rare, but not totally unheard of. 'The customer is always right' in the sense that if he doesn't like what he is offered he has the inalienable right to cease to be a customer. But just once in a while any organisation may, for valid reasons, exercise its right not to be a supplier.

If such a situation is at all likely, it is best to have rules, and to make them widely known. Justice that is seen to be impartial is far more likely to be accepted with a good grace.

If such a situation arises unexpectedly, then the best that can be hoped for is a clean, quick divorce accepted by both parties as inevitable.

Thought-starters

1. Have your customer-contact staff been abused and exploited by customers? If so, how, and what steps were taken to avoid a recurrence?
2. Is customer dishonesty a problem in your business? If so, what forms does it take, and what can be done about it? Is there a danger that these measures might damage the goodwill of other customers?
3. Does your organisation get the type of customer it aims to get? If not, what action might help?
4. Have you ever been 'miscast' as an awkward customer? If so, what were the circumstances, and how might it reasonably have been avoided? Have you ever become aware that you have miscast a customer or seen your staff do so? If so, why did it happen and how might it be avoided?
5. What provision, if any, does your organisation make for customers with a disability? Should it do more?
6. Have you as an individual, or your organisation, ever rejected a customer? If so, why, what was the customer's reaction, and do you think the action was right?

Action points

1. Take all necessary precautions to ensure safety from attack of front-line staff (page 67).
2. Brief and train front-line staff to recognise and help customers suffering from disability or illness (page 69).
3. Upgrade your own treatment of seemingly and truly awkward customers (pages 69-75).

6
BETTER COMMUNICATIONS

THE POSTMAN OF a small Derbyshire village had a busy morning. There was no room in his sack for ordinary letters, as it was completely filled with identical buff envelopes. Every house got its share. Typical was one house that got four; addressed to the father, to the mother, the six-year-old daughter, and the three-year-old son.

Inside each envelope was an identical, duplicated letter. The father and mother read theirs; the daughter struggled a bit with some of the words; the son didn't make very much of it when it was read to him. The letter, from the district health authority, stated that one of the local GPs had retired, that he was being replaced by another doctor, and that patients who didn't want to go to the new doctor had the right to choose another. Both parents already knew these facts; neither child was interested.

Gross over-communication of this type is, thankfully, relatively rare. The common case is under-communication.

How much do they know?

The overwhelming need for information at virtually all stages of the customer service sequence was explained in Chapter 2. If we are to give good service, we must communicate and go on communicating with our customers and potential customers.

One of the first steps to effective communication is to gain an accurate picture of the state of the other party's knowledge, biases and preconceptions.

Customers' knowledge varies widely, so we will always have some work to do on this first phase. Experts do not like being patronised and treated like beginners; beginners are confused and frustrated by the jargon and complexities suitable for communicating with experts.

Face-to-face communication allows interaction from which this can be readily assessed; written and telephonic communication is less effective; mass communication is least effective of all.

If we do not know what customers know, it may be important to try to find out. This will be part of the customer service survey (Chapter 13), but it may be undertaken as a separate exercise at any time. Depending on how many customers we have, and how often we meet them (if at all), we may decide to conduct a survey by questionnaire (handed to customers, included with goods, posted or inserted in a journal or magazine), by telephone, or by face-to-face interview.

A survey of this sort is quite simple to undertake, although the design of the questionnaire will need careful thought. It should not be so long that it is tedious to use, nor so short that it does not cover the important areas. It should either lead from easy questions to harder ones or follow some straightforward sequence. Questions should be simply and clearly worded, without ambiguity. They should be open, and not force answers or guide the respondents towards what we would like them to say.

In designing the questionnaire, consider how the information can be analysed and used when you have it. Always try out questionnaires; first on yourself and your co-workers, then on a small sample of customers. Feed back improvements as you go along, and retest before you finalise the design.

Some organisations offer a small reward for completion in order to stimulate the response rate: either a small sample, a voucher or perhaps a chance to participate in a competition.

If we are also concerned to learn about the knowledge of potential customers, the survey will be more complex, as it will involve planning and reaching a suitable sample of the general public. If we do not have the services of a marketing department, we may want to employ specialist market research consultants to help with such a survey.

Means of communication

There are more means of communication with the customer than we sometimes remember.

Face-to-face letter and telephone communication are the most frequent, and each of these has a separate section. But there are many others, which may be appropriate for particular phases in the customer service sequence. Here are some:

- Pre-ordering information
- Customer panels
- Talks to clubs etc
- Customer suggestion schemes
- Customer directors/board-level advocates
- Customer advisers/counsellors/personal contacts
- Calendars/diaries
- Published company information
- Open days/organised visits
- Exchange visits
- Packing slips
- Instruction manuals
- Hotlines/advice bureaux
- Customer training

Pre-ordering information
Telling customers what goods or services are available and how to get them is closely related to, but essentially different from, selling.

Good examples of this include college prospectuses and the information leaflets provided by British Rail detailing the types of fares available and the conditions attached to each. Transport timetables also fall in this category, even though recent research on teenagers showed that about 40 per cent were unable to understand them.

Customer panels
As our main aim is always to find out what the customer wants, it is best to communicate with him direct. Some organisations have established standing or *ad hoc* panels of customers to advise them on the customer view of what is currently done or of changes that are being considered. Traditionally this has been the preserve of large organisations, but even small, local organisations may feel the technique is worth trying. It may be surprising how many people will give up half an evening when tempted with the offer of sherry, nuts and the chance to air their views.

Parent-teacher organisations perform functions in this area.

Talks to clubs etc

Some organisations, particularly in the retail field, have grasped the benefits of offering talks to appropriate clubs, institutes and similar organisations. Such talks, which are welcomed with open arms by many an honorary officer with a programme to fill, can offer an ideal method of establishing two-way customer communication on an informative, rather than a selling level. They may be particularly appropriate for service organisations such as public leisure facilities, transport, health and education.

Such talks form a natural opportunity for simple customer training (eg 'How to use a timetable') as part of more comprehensive sessions.

Customer suggestion schemes

A customer suggestion box is quite easy to use. While it will always be misused by an irresponsible minority, the potential benefits can be highly cost-effective. Such schemes often offer prizes or gifts for suggestions accepted.

Customer directors/board-level advocates

One or two organisations in both public and private sectors have found a specific customer presence at board level to be helpful.

Customer advisers/counsellors/personal contacts

In many organisations, as soon as the sale is made, the customer is left without any known point of contact with the supplier. All too often each step through the customer service sequence brings a new point of contact: salesman, order clerk, progress chaser, delivery driver, complaints department, service department, accounts clerk etc.

Some suppliers have come to the conclusion that a customer service department which has the specific mission of forming a constant point of reference throughout the service sequence does a lot to improve communication with customers.

At least one major bank has established a system of 'personal bankers' under which a nominated member of staff is responsible for and known as the principal point of contact with each customer.

Calendars/diaries

Many organisations use calendars, diaries, year planning charts and the like for selling purposes. They can be used for customer communication by printing organisation charts, names, addresses and phone numbers (perhaps even photographs) of customer-contact staff, and other advice about contact in the different phases of a transaction. Such an approach may even prove, indirectly, to be a far more powerful selling instrument than direct advertising copy.

Published company information
Some organisations, particularly the large and complex, produce a brochure describing all aspects of their operation of relevance to customers, together with contact details.

To reply automatically to all requests for information with a copy of the latest Annual Report is usually of little help.

Open days/organised visits
To walk round an organisation, seeing the ambience in which it operates, is a powerful form of communication, with many intangible but real benefits. Such opportunities are often given as a means of direct selling, particularly in operations that are of obvious visual interest such as potteries or glass factories. There may be many other organisations which could consider this technique as an aid to customer relations.

Exchange visits
To write to someone, or speak to them regularly on the telephone, leaves many gaps in a relationship and many chances of misunderstanding and failed communication. It may be well worth making a rule that any regular business contacts (eg order clerk/buyer, etc) are always cemented at an early stage by the exchange of visits.

Packing slips
The conventional packing slip may be deliberately anonymous, giving only a number to be quoted in case of complaint. Some organisations have found advantage in specifically personal slips even (in a few cases) with photographs of the people concerned. It may help to give a feeling of pride of workmanship as well as strengthening customer contact.

It may even be felt worthwhile for those assembling or making hardware to attach their personal name label to it. In the right situation, this might work magic by re-establishing a sense of personal contact between maker and user.

Instruction manuals

The manuals supplied for the computer/word processor on which this book was written were almost unusable. They clearly consisted of four or five separate, in some cases overlapping, manuals that have been rapidly thrown together in new binders. Some sections were written in a manner that my experienced systems analyst wife found hard to disentangle; other sections adopted such an elementary approach that a tyro such as the writer felt patronised and insulted. The purpose and use of many of the features of the machine were described in such involved or incomplete fashion as to make them totally unusable. There were several separate indexes and tables of contents buried in the depths of the pages; how to find them was as difficult as deciding which to use. Were it not for the insight of my teenage son, I would long ago have gone back to my typewriter.

The later issues of this manual were much improved. Sadly, some of the best-known software companies have not learnt this lesson and continue to produce manuals which record the ingenuity of their designers but do absolutely nothing for the user except confuse.

Awareness of the importance of user instructions in giving customer service appears to vary enormously. In many cases, such as this computer, they have clearly not been taken seriously, but thrown together as an afterthought. But features of a product (or service) which are so badly described that the customer does not know how to use them, or get the best out of them, may just as well not exist.

Suppliers who regard such things as an optional extra may need to reflect on the effect on customer satisfaction, brand loyalty and future sales of a product that is misused or not used to full advantage by the customer.

Hotlines/advice bureaux

A telephone hotline from which advice can be obtained on products or services may be very helpful, provided customers know it exists. It will need to be open during all hours and days of the week in which customers are most likely to use the product and its existence widely advertised. It is naturally linked to a bureau from which customers are encouraged to obtain written advice.

There is an important distinction between reaction and proaction; customers need to be made aware that they are welcome to use such facilities, that they are something that comes automatically with the product, not merely answers reluctantly given to those prepared to make a nuisance of themselves.

Customer training
Rolls-Royce and similar high-technology organisations have for many years operated customer training schools, for those who will have to use or maintain their products.

Other, less specialised organisations might find benefit from a similar approach; it is a very costly solution, but may be more cost-effective in the long run than trying to sell a product which is then misused by customers.

In time of trouble

From the departure lounge, passengers were herded on to the airport bus. After a circuitous trip round the tarmac, they stood for ten minutes while the driver and a member of the aircrew conferred. Without a word, the driver re-entered, and drove slowly back by a different route. Once back, he left the passengers sardined in his bus while he entered the terminal. At length, a few of the braver passengers followed him, to find that he and the stewardess had been replaced by two burly security officers, who ordered them perfunctorily back on to the bus.

The ticket barrier to the tube was suddenly shut, and within a few minutes a growing, milling and dangerous crowd of would-be homeward bound commuters had gathered. No member of staff was to be seen. No one was attempting to stem the flow at the top of the steps. No advice was available as to what had happened, whether it was serious, how long it might last, or whether there were alternative routes.

Airports, bus stations, railway and tube stations often leave passengers standing helplessly without information. But they are not the only villains.

Some garages do not tell the customer that they have run out of the necessary parts, or that they have hit some other snag and have not completed the repair until the hapless customer arrives to collect. ('Well, you could always have rung us to find out how we were doing...'.) Shops, or suppliers at any level in the supply chain, often offer no information about delays to orders until asked, and then only with reluctance. The list is endless and appalling.

Failure to communicate with customers at times of difficulty is one of the biggest and worst of customer service errors.

Pro-active and reactive communication

If an order (or a plane, or a doctor) has been delayed, the worst thing is to tell the customer (or the passenger, or the patient) nothing. But the next worst is to tell him only what he asks for.

This is inadequate for several reasons; it conveys an uncaring, possibly arrogant impression; it appears inefficient; it seems defensive. Information which has been volunteered has a completely different feel from the same information wrung from someone like blood from a stone. Many customers will be reluctant to ask. Some will not know which questions to ask, or who to ask them of. All will feel upset.

This is also a matter of self-defence for the supplier. The party that initiates a communication seizes an advantage, whatever the situation. It has a psychological advantage, and can set the tone (friendly, helpful, positive). It has a formal advantage, and can provide a framework for the exchange, directing attention towards certain aspects and away from others. It has a personal advantage, and can choose who is to give and who to receive the communication. A party that says nothing until asked loses all these.

The supplier should, in any case, be aware of the problem before the customer, and therefore be in a position to warn of, or possibly prevent him suffering, problems.

For all these reasons, communication, particularly about delays and difficulties, should be pro-active; the supplier should initiate it.

Thought-starters

1. Have you ever suffered from over-communication by an organisation (including your own)? If so, what happened, why did it happen, and what harm was caused?
2. What (in general terms) would you like your customers and potential customers to know about your organisation, how it works, and what it offers?

3. What do your customers and potential customers (a) know, (b) possibly know, and (c) probably not know that you would like them to know?
4. How do you know what your customers and potential customers know and do not know? Would surveys be (a) beneficial, and (b) practicable?
5. What means does your organisation use to communicate with customers in each phase of the customer service sequence?
6. Are there any phases in the sequence in which your communication may be weak? If so, what do you feel would be worth considering as means of improving it?
7. Does your organisation volunteer information to customers if something has gone wrong (eg a delay)? If not, (a) would it help, and (b) would it be practicable?

Action points

1. Consider setting up customer panels (page 79).
2. Arrange to give talks to clubs, societies and institutes (page 80).
3. Start a customer suggestions scheme (page 80).
4. Produce customer-contact diaries/calendars (pages 80-81).
5. Organise a customer Open Day (page 81).
6. Set up exchange visits with regular customers for all customer-contact staff (page 81).
7. Produce and use personalised packing slips (page 81).
8. Check and revise all user instruction manuals and leaflets (page 82).
9. Set up and make known an advice hotline for customers (page 82).
10. Consider giving customer training (page 83).
11. Set up an order-status hotline and a procedure to advise customers as soon as likely delays become known (pages 83-4).

7
LETTER WRITING

WE ARE ALL rather less literate than we might think. Writing and reading are advanced and demanding skills, and if there are easier ways of doing things, most of us will choose them. The proportion of business which organisations conduct by letter has probably been falling slowly and continuously over several decades.

The effect of technology

The effect of the typewriter on letter writing would probably bear study. It seems possible that interposing the apparatus of typewriter, typing pool, shorthand and secretary between the correspondent and his letter has resulted in delay and perhaps a reluctance to write that was not felt when all that was needed was to pick up pen and paper. A surprising amount of delay can occur through the nuts and bolts of letter production; transmitting the text for typing, typing, getting it back, correcting, sending to the post room, etc. These details may easily add three days to the reply cycle for correspondence, sometimes much more.

The procedure of having letters typed has probably also tended to make letters less effective communicators; the style is probably less spontaneous, more complex and pompous than it would have been if we hand wrote the letters ourselves. The replacement of typing by word-processing by the writer may, in the longer term, reverse this process.

As the telephone has become readily available, it has been used more and more in place of letters. In the early days, telephone conversations were always confirmed by letter. This is still frequent, especially when money and meeting arrangements are involved, but more rare in other situations.

It may be that facsimile transmission will lead to an increase in letter writing once again.

The increased availability of office copiers and duplicators has resulted in a massive increase in the number of circulars and the rise of the whole category of 'junk mail'. No one has found an answer to this; we all produce more year by year, but as the volume increases, the reading and response rate drops.

'Dear Miss Smith,' ran the smartly typed letter, 'Your birthday on 16 January will soon be here and prior to that special day, you must decide whether or not you wish to take this once only opportunity to review your family's life insurance requirements when the cost will be calculated at your current age of 50...

'As of the date of this correspondence, I have not received your completed application form and I am, therefore, contacting you again to recommend that you give serious consideration to taking advantage of your right to apply for this important protection at this time.

'Irrespective of your decision, Miss Smith, please have a great day on 16 January.

'Yours very sincerely, etc'

Word processors can now generate in personal form what are nothing more than circulars, and to most recipients, junk mail. This is a pity, as it further debases the whole process of correspondence. Good customer relations demand that this facility should be used sparingly.

Effective letters

The steps to effective letter writing are not difficult; a little thought and practice can make a big improvement. Here are some suggestions:

Read carefully

If we do not read well, there is little chance that we will write a good reply. Effective communication depends on both the sending and receiving being accurate; many a carefully thought-out reply has gone wrong because it failed to answer the questions the customer actually asked.

Nothing is easier than to misread, particularly if our emotions are involved, as they may be by apparent criticism, what seems to be an unreasonable request, rudeness or sarcasm, or by failure to read *our* previous letter.

The use of a coloured text highlighter can help in the process of reading and understanding, and it certainly helps to ensure that all material points are emphasised for easy discussion with colleagues and for later reading and reply.

Decide how to reply
Like leading or not leading trumps in bridge, the choice between a letter, a phone call or perhaps a meeting is easy to misjudge.

The best way to reply to a letter may not be to write back. A phone call may be better for speed, to correct some misunderstanding, to establish closer personal contact, to avoid putting delicate or difficult matters or for other reasons. Sometimes a face-to-face meeting may be the best response.

Reply speedily
Napoleon said that he never replied to letters because in the end all letters answered themselves.

Sadly, none of us is Napoleon. Far and away the commonest customer complaint about letters is that replies are tardy, and if the pile of letters in the in-tray is for ever growing, something needs to be done.

Return of post is best; work does not get any less by being left. A loaded in-tray suggests a heavy workload, but may simply arise from habit. If the amount in arrears remains fairly steady, taking one day (or week, as appropriate) with the next, the cause is unlikely to be overloading. If the volume in arrears fluctuates fairly regularly from none to a lot and back, the problem is probably peaked or irregular arrival causing queueing-type difficulties. There may be some way of using extra help at peak times to avoid long-term arrears.

Some people accumulate arrears subconsciously, to give a feeling of security through being wanted; there is always a pile needing our attention, and to come in to an empty desk and in-tray would be to feel naked. They may even be accumulated deliberately, in order to give the impression of overload or indispensability. Such sad events do not help the customer or the business he wants to bring us.

Delay may occur legitimately through the need to obtain information with which to reply. In this case, we will probably want to send an immediate acknowledgement. However, if this happens regularly it suggests that some aspect of the work needs examination. It may be that other departments do not realise that customer contact is involved, or have not understood the need for speed.

As has been said, the process of getting letters typed may add days on to the time taken; the typing pool may have a queueing problem too.

In some circumstances, it may be better to give an immediate handwritten reply than risk a delay due to typing. This also offers the advantages of cheapness and the personal touch; if a letter is handwritten, there can be no doubt it has received our personal attention. The obvious desire for speed may impress a customer more than a well-typed but delayed reply.

The use of a word processor or a personal computer at a self-contained workstation offers advantages to everyone handling customer correspondence and is worth examining even in smaller organisations or units. It need not be costly; the equivalent may not cost more than a month's salary of the person using it. With such equipment on their desk, writers can retain control of all aspects of letter production and eliminate the delay of moving work about the building.

Use of a word processor may be combined with use of standard letters covering situations which arise frequently. These can be adapted to meet individual cases, and run off as personal letters. This process can be useful even without a word processor.

The word processor can be a great help in personalising correspondence. Customers do not like what are obviously stereotyped letters; the word processor allows every letter to be produced as if it were original and personal. However, over-use of this equipment, especially for selling, can in the end become offensive and counter-productive, and merely create more junk mail.

Excuses, excuses

If delay has occurred, and the customer complains, such hoary chestnuts such as 'It's in type' and 'It's in the post' don't cut much ice. The first admits a lack of managerial control—I can't get important letters typed in less than a day or two. The second might be used if it happens to be true, but customers who have been told this have a nasty habit of looking at the postmark when at last the letter arrives. If the postal service is that bad (and all too often it is) then the good manager will have opened discussions with the Post Office.

Person to person

Both the content and production of letters to customers ought to show that the organisation knows and treats them as individuals.

Letters should usually be replied to by the person written to; if this is not sensible (because that person has left, or changed jobs, or was not the best person to help the customer) this should be explained at the start of the reply.

Some senior executives pass letters from less important customers to subordinates for reply. If challenged, most would claim that this is a matter of simple necessity; if they tried to reply personally to everything they would have insufficient time and would, in any case end up doing their subordinates' jobs for them.

A few executives (or possibly their secretaries) may regard personal reply as a matter of status rather than function. This is a pity, as it might harm, or at least miss a chance to improve, customer relations and perhaps to do extra business.

Be simple

The old-fashioned, flowery language of business has long ago been killed off. But its ghost still lingers about phrases like 'the above instruction', 'dissatisfaction with the same' and others. They are best avoided.

There is always a temptation to try to impress the reader, by using long and important-sounding words and phrases. But our aim should always be to express our meaning by choosing the simplest and most direct words that will do so. The aim should never be to sound important, and always be to communicate effectively.

Be brief

The Churchillian adage 'put it on one sheet of paper' remains as sound as ever it was. Another wise saying goes, 'If I'd had more time, I'd have written less.'

There are not all that many business situations which really call for a letter of more than one sheet. Even if they do, the problems most people have in reading lengthy documents mean that they are likely to remain unread or only partly understood. If we must write at length, it helps the reader to use paragraph headings and tabular form whenever possible, and put detail into an appendix.

It is certainly not cheating to use diagrams, graphs and pictures if they will help to express our meaning; one picture is worth a thousand words.

The rule of brevity applies down the chain: short paragraphs, short sentences and short words. There are occasions when the rule must be broken, to avoid a harsh, staccato style; but it remains a good general rule.

Avoid jargon

We may have a special difficulty if our trade or profession uses a language of its own. Avoiding jargon is not easy, but some trades seem more prone than others; printers, builders and computer experts, for example, have to exercise particular care.

Jargon has two legitimate functions; it expresses concepts that may be difficult or lengthy to express in common language, and it helps to form a bond between those who share (or want to be thought to share) the same expertise.

If we are writing to a customer who is an expert, we will probably want to use jargon; if not, we should try to avoid it. If we are not sure which is the case, it is probably rather better to risk sounding patronising by avoiding jargon than to risk misunderstanding by using it. Best of all must be to establish which is true at the earliest stage, perhaps by a suitable telephone discussion or meeting.

Avoid bad usage

Bad grammar, punctuation and spelling, and incorrect usage of words or phrases in a written document are best avoided. Some people, including some customers, may regard grammar as old-fashioned. But if you flout accepted grammatical usage in a letter to a customer you can be sure your sins will find you out. Occasionally, a customer may take such a pleasure from showing off his knowledge and educating us that our mistake may make us a friend for life, but it is not wise to count on such luck.

Many people rely on their secretaries or typists for such things. Luckily, most secretaries and typists are quite good at them, and willing to help, especially with spelling. But correct English usage still has traps, and unless we are prepared to spend time consulting reference books, it is probably better to avoid anything about which we have the slightest doubt; English is, luckily, a language of many alternatives.

Be accurate

After delay, customers complain most about letters that are factually inaccurate.

Even trivial inaccuracies must be avoided; mistakes with dates, names etc may not appear to matter, but they give an impression of carelessness which is bad for business.

One of the worst of trivial mistakes is to mistake or misspell the customer's name. Reading signatures is often tricky but always important. Our name is one of our most intimate properties, and errors with it can give great offence. They suggest (usually quite unfairly, of course, but the mind is not rational in such matters) lack of recognition of us as people. The same is true, to a lesser extent, of mistakes with company names. Rolls-Royce employees, for example, may get very upset if written to without the hyphen. Companies with the status of 'plc' may be offended if addressed as 'Ltd'.

Occasionally, the discovery of trivial inaccuracies has led to the opening out of far more serious matters as, for example, when a calculation has been based on a wrong rate of discount.

Be complete

Failure to reply to questions or points raised by customers is another frequent grouse.

Deliberate omissions are one thing, but simply failing to answer a question, or to give essential information, is another and much more serious fault. This should not happen; customers' letters should be read thoroughly and replied to point by point.

Avoid discourtesy

Nothing is more tempting than to reply to rudeness with rudeness, but nothing in business must be resisted more strongly. Feelings such as, 'We can't be expected to take that one lying down,' or perhaps 'What if we do upset old X—his business doesn't matter anyway,' are temptations from the devil, as we shall rapidly find out when our reply is shown round the golf club, or ends up on our chairman's desk, or maybe our solicitor's...

Another temptation to be resisted is to use sarcasm and innuendo. Innuendos that seem subtle when we wrote them in our office have a habit of reading like blatant rudeness when we next see them lying on the chairman's desk. At the least, we should seek a reliable second opinion before sending, preferably from the boss. After all, what are bosses for?

Another trap may be to write something which, or in a way which, upsets a particular customer. We may think we know how someone will react, but misjudge him. We may be accused of over-familiarity, or fail to take seriously something we thought was intended as a throw-away comment. A letter is a record for all to see, and lacks the feedback and opportunity for correction of mistakes offered by a face-to-face meeting.

To release tension and righteous anger, some write the rudest reply they can, tear it into small pieces, and throw it into the waste paper basket. For a particularly provocative and unpleasant customer, this may need repeating several times before the draft is suitable to send.

A sensible and mature tactic in many such situations is to telephone the writer and either try to sort the problem out then and there, or to arrange a meeting at which that can be done. Sometimes, there may be situations in which this is unsuitable; if previous contact has already fully explored the problem, if personal relationships are particularly bad, if there are other people involved, or if the matter might go to law, for example.

When all has been said and done, the best way to avoid an impression of rudeness is to write a simple, straightforward and friendly letter, pretending (if pretence is actually necessary) that we like and value the customer as a person.

Editing
Most people find editing a great deal easier than writing. It is even easy to edit other people's work; bringing a fresh mind to bear is a great help. Writers who are not too possessive about their letters can sometimes gain a great deal by passing them to a colleague for editing. If this is impracticable, we must edit our own work mercilessly.

Signature
The potential embarrassment from a misread signature has already been mentioned; we must always do our bit to avoid this by ensuring our signature is followed by our typed name.

Some organisations have a problem as to who should sign letters and in what form. Should all letters to the public be signed by departmental heads? Should they be signed 'for' the company? Should they be signed with surname and initials, first name and surname, initials only? Should job titles be used? Should qualifications or decorations be given? May letters be 'pp'd'? Can they be signed in the writer's absence, and if so in what form?

There are no universal rules about such things, but common sense may suggest some pointers.

The difficulty experienced by customers who have many points of contact with an organisation suggests that letters should be signed by one specific individual who can be contacted in other ways (face-to-face or by phone); the contact should be direct and personal. If customer service has been put in the hands of one department, this problem should be solved.

Today, first names and surnames are increasingly used in all contacts, and no longer felt to be too intimate or too Americanised. However, female writers who do this may cause doubt as to what greeting to use in a reply if they do not indicate whether they prefer 'Mrs', 'Miss', or 'Ms'. Job titles often help the customer by indicating the place in the organisation and the degree of authority of the person writing. There are very few occasions indeed in which qualifications or decorations should be added.

The prime need to avoid delay suggests that there should always be a mechanism to despatch letters in the writer's absence. 'Pping' is not very satisfactory, as it may convey the flavour of a subordinate dealing with a matter of minor importance, and at the least does nothing to explain why the supposed writer did not sign himself. Better is probably the time-honoured formula 'Dictated by X and signed in his absence'. Some will even recommend a forged signature on a letter that is known to have the writer's full authority.

Final production

The letter as sent should be well laid out, free from mistakes and corrections. Some of us are not specially good at proof-reading, but it is an essential discipline; if we fail to spot the mistake, the customer will.

It is, of course, essential to check figures; recalling or correcting a wrong quotation is almost certain to lose a customer, unless it happens to be lower than it should have been, which may keep the customer but lose us our job.

Thought-starters

1. Do you write many letters in your job? Is this way of working

a conscious decision, or has it just happened? If it was a decision, what were your reasons? Would the job benefit from writing more or less?

2. Does your correspondence get into arrears; if so, what is the reason? What (apart from occasional unforeseen problems) stops you from replying to letters the same day?

3. How are your letters produced? Does the system work well, or might handwritten memos, use of a desk-top word processor, use of standard letters or some other change help?

4. Do you ever look back at the letters you write to see whether they might have been made more effective? If so, could they, and does this suggest anything about the way you write that you might change to make a permanent improvement?

5. Have you ever seriously upset a customer by a letter you have written? If so, what has the episode taught you?

Action points

1. Establish return-of-post reply norm (page 88).
2. Provide desk-top word processors for staff with extensive customer correspondence (page 89).
3. Set up standard letter formats to cover common situations (page 89).
4. Upgrade your own letter writing skills and those of your staff (pages 87-94).

8
THE TELEPHONE

UNLESS WE HAVE a business (such as retailing) in which most customers walk through the front door, the telephone is likely to be our most important instrument of customer service.

The telephone becomes more important year by year. The growing use of car phones and telephone answering machines and further technical development will probably keep up the momentum for a long time to come.

More transactions are now completed on the telephone; while confirmation in writing will always be necessary in specific cases, telephone appointments and orders are increasingly accepted as sufficient in themselves.

For these reasons, selecting, training, guiding and cherishing telephonists and telephone users is likely to be one of the most important actions that can be taken to improve our customer service. It is incomprehensible that some organisations will spend fortunes on sales campaigns, but save pennies on these vital links in the chain of service.

Five steps to effective use of the phone

Many obstacles may be put in the way of efficient telephone performance by the organisation. These five steps should help your telephonist, and through him, everyone else:

1. Get good equipment
Getting the best from your telephonist begins by giving him the best and most suitable equipment the organisation can afford. Telephone technology has advanced rapidly, and is continuing to do so. Organisations who try to save by using inefficient and out-

dated equipment will probably lose heavily from the damage to customer relations and lost business opportunities.

Modern equipment, with its many facilities for such things as the storage of calls and numbers, diversion and transfer under many conditions, can do a lot to smooth customer contact.

Because of problems of peak demand, there are some organisations which face particularly severe difficulties in rapid answering of calls. These include railway enquiry offices, doctors' surgeries and others. Much customer goodwill can be lost in such situations, and with it business opportunities. As with any queueing problems, solutions may be hard to find and may involve money, but the money will be very well spent. A solution now technically available is the automatic diversion of calls, perhaps to a less busy location or to a telephone answering bureau that can handle the routine enquiries that often form the bulk of calls, and pass messages to the appropriate office about the remainder.

It is possible to get equipment that will play a recorded message assuring callers that they will receive an answer as soon as possible, or even play nice music. However, such messages cost both parties money, and are usually felt to achieve little.

Once obtained, the organisation's telephone equipment should be installed in the best location for effective use. This may be away from distractions; but it may, depending on the size and nature of the organisation, be where the telephonist can see where people are and what they are doing.

2. Give technical training
Full training in the technical use of the equipment is usually provided when it is first installed. This may not happen if it is taken over as part of a new office, when a new telephonist is appointed, or for relief telephonists.

All users of extensions (which usually means everyone in the building) will also need training in the correct technical use of their equipment. The many features of a modern telephone installation are likely to remain unused, or to be used incorrectly, if everyone involved is not told, encouraged and trained in their use.

3. Structure the job right
The telephonist's job must be structured properly.

The telephonist must not be encumbered with other duties that make it impossible to work effectively. The common combination of telephonist and receptionist only works well when there are few calls or few visitors. If not, there is the risk that both important jobs will be badly done, with consequent damage to customer service.

Because of the specialised and often physically isolated nature of their work, many telephonists may get little by way of support and guidance from management. The principal objectives for telephonists are often said to be speed and accuracy in handling calls, but their role in effective customer service suggests that warm helpfulness should be added to the top of the list. The aim must not be speed at any price, and symptoms of over-loading must be spotted early and treated as a serious danger signal.

Telephonists' working hours are also important to customer relations. The normal office hours may not necessarily be best. The question to be answered is: what are the important times for customer contact? Some businesses may gain a vital marketing advantage by offering a full 24-hour service.

4. Establish good discipline

Adequate systems and disciplines for telephone use are essential.

These should include guidance on any purposes for which the telephone should not be used, on the use of off-peak time, the handling of calls when people are not available and dealing with calls from outside staff.

They should also include guidance about incoming and outgoing personal calls. Such calls incur not only the direct cost, but occupy telephone lines, equipment and staff time. However, rules that are too tight or impracticable may prove unenforceable and only cause resentment. Some organisations provide booths from which private calls may be made. The installation of a call-monitoring machine is now easy, and will probably cover its costs, if only by its deterrent effect.

5. Behavioural training

Besides technical training, both telephonists and users need training in the behavioural aspects of telephone use.

Because telephonist and users are part of a team when handling calls, it is particularly valuable that they should, like other teams, occasionally meet and train together. In large organisations in particular, telephonists are often physically isolated from users. Bringing them together now and then for short training sessions, or on switchboard open days, may do a lot to aid mutual under-standing and smooth out both technical and personal problems.

Many of the skills of using the telephone are common to tele-phonist, secretary and other users; some are specific to the job. The following list is split by job, but each section includes sugges-tions that may be helpful to any user.

Suggestions for the telephonist

Speed of reply

We all have a built-in picture of someone at the other end of a tele-phone line calmly doing a manicure or finishing a cup of coffee while we are kept waiting. Every second a phone is allowed to go on ringing beyond the first three or four rings increases the tension of the caller, and stores up potential problems. At the least, these will make it harder to establish quick and easy rapport with the caller; at the most, they will make him abort the call and take his business elsewhere.

'The first three or four rings' is suggested as most people feel startled if a call is answered immediately; the caller needs a mom-ent to get his breath.

If the telephonist is too busy to handle a call, most people would prefer that it is not answered until it can be properly dealt with; that way the caller does not have the expense and frustration of hanging on. 'X company, one moment please' is *not* a good formula.

Use of voice

Because it is all the caller has to go on, our voice must immediately convey a wealth of information. We must make clear who we are, what role we have, and the fact that we are alert, warm, friendly, intelligent, knowledgeable and willing to help the caller in any way we can. This is quite a tall order, but it can be done.

'Put a smile in your voice' is perhaps the best summary of what's wanted. Indeed, the very act of smiling is as important in using the phone as in face-to-face contact; it affects the voice immediately, and for the better, and is quite recognisable at the other end of the line.

The other side of this coin is to avoid reacting to an unpleasant or aggressive use of voice by the caller. He may not have our degree of telephone skill or have had the advantage of our training; his wife may have left him that morning, or his son failed his exams; our organisation may just have lost him a big order by a late delivery. Some people, particularly those who do not use the phone frequently, are nervous when they do, and nerves alone may cause someone to sound aggressive.

The greeting
The first words set the tone of the whole conversation.

It is usual to state the name of the organisation—'Smith and Company'—unless more than one organisation is serviced from the same switchboard, in which case the telephone number would usually be stated: 'Emsworth 1234'. These cannot be faulted, *provided*:

(a) The circuit is not opened after the reply has been started;
(b) The words are spoken with such a clarity and at such a pace that the caller can hear them;
(c) The tone of voice is welcoming and friendly, not conveying 'I really am very busy; state your business at once and then get out of my hair'.

'Yup', 'What?', 'Hullo', 'Can I help you' and variants do not go down well with customers.

Recognise people
Nothing gets a contact off on a better basis than immediate recognition of the caller by his voice. 'Yes, of course, Mr Green, I'll put you through,' may be enough to clinch a deal.

Needless to say this immensely valuable technique is dangerous for those who do not have a good ear or memory for voices; mistaken identity is at the best embarrassing and at the worst dangerous.

Don't struggle with a bad line
Say at once if you have difficulty in hearing; don't risk a call going wrong because you have misheard or need to shout at the customer. Remember that bad lines can sometimes be bad one way only. Suggest immediately that the caller rings back.

Tell the caller what you are doing
Remember that clicks and funny noises usually spell trouble on the phone, and if you make one, explain that all is well.

'The line's ringing now', 'Transferring you', etc are helpful and reassuring to the caller, provided it *is* ringing now or they *are* being transferred, and provided the tone of voice makes it clear that we care about the caller very much, and don't regard him as a nuisance to be got rid of as quickly as possible.

Don't disappear
In using the telephone, silence is taken to indicate a problem. The caller can't see what we're up to (mercifully, sometimes) and therefore if we do not respond, or the line goes quiet, he will think we have dropped off to sleep or the line has been lost.

It is important also to leave an extension ringing for the correct length of time; neither too long nor too short. Apart from the sense of abandonment felt by the caller, lengthy ringing disturbs other people in an office, and occupies the switchboard. What the correct length is, only sense and experience will tell; on some extensions, we may know that Bill is often filing at the other side of his office and we must give him time to get across; on others, we may be sure that if Mary does not reply within six rings she's not there.

Take a message
If no extension is able to help the caller, we must offer to take a message. There are one or two organisations that actually instruct their telephonists *not* to take messages. Whilst there may appear to be internal reasons to justify this (such as savings in overloaded telephonists' time) the damage to customer relations must surely heavily outweigh these. Even if alternative message-taking arrangements are available, the negative reactions generated by the surly and unhelpful response 'We are not allowed to take messages,' will be difficult to live down.

For those who do take messages, writing instrument and paper should, of course, be always ready. Many organisations use specially printed message forms, which can be useful as they attract immediate attention when left on a desk (see Figure 5 overleaf).

Good message-taking is quite an art:

1. Write the date *and time* of the call. Time may prove to be important to the recipient, if only to check whether a conversation with the same caller was before or after the message.
2. Write the caller's name, organisation and role if it is volunteered.

Telephone Message

For:			
From:	Name		
	Company		
	Number	STD Code	Ext

Message:

Message: Taken by

Time taken

Date taken

Please ring back ☐   They will ring back ☐

Figure 5. *A telephone message-form*

3. Write the caller's phone number, STD code and extension. Even if the caller is well known to the person being called, they may not always be on their usual number. If they are, it is convenient to have that number on the message. The same applies to the STD code, which is not always volunteered, perhaps because some people are confused as to how it works.
4. Write the message, with as much detail as the caller offers, making as much sense as if you were about to deal with it

yourself. To write a nonsense, on the assumption that the recipient will be able to decode it, will only cause later difficulty, and may result in the caller having to repeat his story later.

5. Ensure the message gets to the recipient. Failure to take care of telephone messages does a lot of harm to customer service. If we are unable to pass it direct to the person concerned, or the message is clearly important or urgent, it may be worth checking that it has been received.

Don't talk to third parties

To talk with others while handling a call is confusing and rude. If something must be said to a third party (for example, another telephonist, a messenger or another caller), the circuit should be closed first. If the discussion lasts more than a few seconds, or if it will have been overheard by the caller, an apology, possibly with a brief explanation, goes down well.

Await reconnection

It is a generally accepted convention that if a connection is lost the caller should call again. It is polite to do this even if a conversation has been virtually concluded, in order to avoid the impression of having slammed the phone down from pique.

Conclude neatly

The conclusion of a call, like the start, is of particular importance, as it is the last thing the caller will remember. It should be particularly warm and friendly, and leave no doubt in the caller's mind as to what has been agreed, and whether the next move will be his or ours.

It is best, as the recipient of a call, to wait for the click at the other end before putting the receiver down.

Secretary

Traditionally, the secretary is the person who stands between the boss and the Outside World, shielding him from annoyance and protecting him from time-wasters. The higher ranking the boss, this view runs, the more tightly his secretary must filter out those attempting to speak to him.

This view of the secretarial role certainly has some truth in it.

For one thing, it can be very helpful to the customer. He may have asked for the Top Person only because he did not know the name or job title of the person who could best help him; if this is so, the secretary will be of great service, having established what he wants, by telling him the name of whoever can best help and transferring him or arranging for him to be called back.

For another, it is a fact that the higher the boss, the more he does need some protection. Annoyed customers invariably set out to address their complaints to the highest manager they can reach, and unless there is some force pulling the other way, then this highest manager must end up taking all the complaints.

However, over-protective secretaries (or those who are seen as over-protective) are a cause of customer frustration and complaint.

The dividing line between necessary protection and over-protectiveness is fine, and takes much judgement. Perhaps the most useful approach is to try to see the situation from the customer's angle. The secretary who makes it clear immediately to each caller that his aim is to be as helpful as possible will actually find it easier to protect his boss, because customers will be more likely to accept diversion if they have confidence it is being suggested in a spirit of helpfulness. This approach may take rather more time with each caller, but it will pay dividends in better customer relations, and may be cancelled out by a reduction in aggression and consequent complaints.

Additional suggestions for the secretarial role include:

Personal greeting
The usual secretarial greeting on the phone is 'Mr Smith's office'. It is worth considering whether a greeting such as 'Mary Jones speaking', or 'Mr Smith's Office, Mary Jones speaking' may be worth experimenting with.

Such greetings imply (perfectly correctly) that Mary Jones is a person of importance in her own right, not just a hurdle on the path to Mr Smith. This is good for Mary, who has the right to such recognition, and it is also helpful for the caller to feel he is speaking to a real person who will be able to help him directly.

Tone of voice
It is an occupational hazard for secretaries, as part of their defensive role, to adopt a deliberately detached and unfriendly tone of voice.

Those who think about it probably feel it establishes authority immediately, and deters frivolous callers. Unfortunately, for every frivolous caller who is cowed by such an approach, there are many more, a lot of them customers or potential customers, whose instinctive reaction to such a tone is hostile. When this happens, they will either give up and take their custom elsewhere, or continue the conversation with what they feel is necessary assertiveness.

A warm and friendly tone is most unlikely, in fact, to encourage time-wasting frivolity; it is more likely to oil the wheels of the conversation, and enable the secretary to get the call into the most suitable channel quickly and smoothly.

The right questions
The way the conversation develops, and how successful it is for both participants, is largely determined by the questioning skill of the secretary. The aim will be to find out quickly and accurately why the caller is phoning; the problem is to do this without putting his back up.

The exact words used can make a big difference. 'May I ask what it's about?' and similar phrases come unstuck with some callers, who see them as inquisitive and interfering. 'Perhaps I can help you?' or a similar question including the word 'help' may prove more effective. The skilled secretary will want to test and develop an approach that suits his personal style.

Assuming that the caller accepts the invitation to explain their reason for calling, the effective secretary will need to pursue skilled and economical questioning to reach the heart of the matter quickly. Even more important than speed is thoroughness; transferring a call to a wrong person causes much frustration and annoyance; should such a thing happen more than once during the same call (and it does), a customer may be lost for ever.

Transferring a call
Transferring a call needs skill. A good sequence might be:

1. Speak to the transferee, and explain what is wanted by the caller.
2. Check that he is able and willing to help.
3. Tell him the name, organisation and position of the caller.
4. Tell the caller the name and position of the person to whom you are transferring him, and the extension number in case he is cut off during transfer.

For all telephone users, quick access to information is important, and a list of telephone extension numbers should always be to hand. Such a list can be supplied to regular customers, or included in some other source of information such as calendars, diaries or catalogues.

Talking about the boss
If the invitations to explain the reason for calling, or to be transferred, are declined (and sometimes in other circumstances) it will be necessary to say something about our boss.

Traditional statements include 'He's in conference', 'He's not in', 'He has somebody with him', 'He's in a meeting', 'He's taking a late lunch', 'He's with clients'. These may be accurate and necessary, but should never be the end of the story.

For one thing, they offer a second chance to help the caller by inviting him to accept transfer to someone else. If, however, this is finally declined, it is very helpful to indicate how long he will be away or engaged. To say merely 'He's not here' leaves the situation wide open; is he in gaol, in the loo, in South America, or has he disappeared without trace? Will he be a month, or a couple of minutes?

Secretary to secretary
When a secretary answers the call of another secretary whose boss wishes to speak to his boss, it is important to avoid a power struggle of precedence—'Who goes through first?'—one simple solution, if both bosses are there, is to say 'Shall we go through together?'

The end
At the end of it all, we must ensure that we and the caller agree how matters are left. Are we calling them back? Is our boss calling them? Is someone else calling them? Are we (or someone) finding them some answers first? Are we passing a message? Are we (or someone) putting something in the post? Is the matter now resolved?

It goes without saying that it is imperative that all these promises are kept, and kept as quickly as possible: calls back the same day; letters in the post that evening.

Some secretaries automatically encourage callers to do the calling back. If they are certain it is a nuisance call, this is as good as anything; in most other circumstances, and always if it is or might be a customer, we should call them.

Other users

Almost everything that has been said about secretaries and telephonists is true for the rest of us, but there are even some additional rules:

Be there
To be unavailable on the telephone may not feel like a crime, but in terms of customer relations it can be a serious offence. We should always make proper arrangements for handling calls when we are out of our office, and check every so often that they are working. When customers start calling us the 'Scarlet Pimpernel' then we should know the battle is virtually lost.

Other people's phones
Other people's phones often cause a problem; they have a nasty habit of ringing when you are the only person around. Of course, you can always ignore it. But if one of our principal concerns is good customer service, it is a problem we must grasp; if it is a customer or potential customer ringing, his future business may depend on your reaction. Quite often it may turn out to be for you anyway.

Identify yourself
The way we start sets the tone of the whole conversation.

'Yup', 'Hallo', 'Order office', 'Smith', 'John Smith', 'John Smith speaking', 'How can I help you?', (silence, except for sound of conversation in background), 'One minute please', 'Hold the line, please', and any known combination of these may be used.

'Yup', 'Hallo' and similar starts do not say who we are or what we do. The caller is driven (unless he happens to know us well, which we cannot count on) to follow up by questioning us to find these things out. He also starts with the feeling we are not used to answering the phone, and may either not be who he wants, or not very good at our job. Moreover, such a start is curt, and unlikely to convey the various positive messages about our personality and intentions that we want.

Whether we use first name and surname or surname only is a matter for the individual, but the tendency for some years has been to use both together; many people today feel that surname alone sounds curt and unfriendly. Some women feel more comfortable introducing themselves as 'Mrs' or 'Miss' X; others see this as sexist or unnecessarily formal. The use of 'Mr' in self-introduction has virtually disappeared. In all cases, it is necessary to speak distinctly, especially if one has a single syllable name such as Peel. We must also hide any resentment we may feel when people hear our names wrongly.

If the office has more than one person who may answer, it is usual to give the name of the office first; 'Order office, Malcolm Peel speaking'.

The caller should, of course, identify himself. It is a good idea to jot down the name, organisation and other information at once as he speaks. It is rude to have to ask for a repetition, but impressive and helps to establish rapport if we use his name during and at the end of the conversation. If he does not introduce himself, a courteous enquiry ('May I ask who is speaking?') has got to be in order.

If someone is with us

'I'm sorry, I'm in a meeting at the moment', will cause most callers to clear the line very rapidly. The picture of their conversation being overheard by a roomful of flapping ears deters all but the most determined of conversationalists. Indeed, the less friendly their intentions, the less they will want to be overheard and perhaps misinterpreted. (It is, of course, worth remembering that a meeting often has as few as two people in it.)

'Sorry, I'm interviewing' is even more certain to deter a caller. But this, of course, conveys such an impression of inefficiency it should never be used merely to get rid of a caller, far less ever actually be allowed to happen.

If we do have someone with us the best tactics are usually to make a normal introduction followed at once by an apology and an offer to ring them back. This is much better than to try to continue and convey the impression they are interrupting something and only have half our ear.

Note it down

It can be useful to keep notes of important telephone conversations, either in a daybook or on file notes or both. As with notes of meetings, this will act as a memory-jogger and also provide evidence, if it is ever needed, of what transpired. It can be shattering and salutary to compare our recollection of a discussion with the notes we took at the time.

Help all

There are few more certain ways to lose potential customers and infuriate existing ones than to pass them from one extension to another, whether because there is no reply, or because the person answering cannot help.

It is surprising how often we are able to answer a query from outside, even when it is not our department. Such answers should, of course follow the information that it *isn't* our department, and that we will tell Mr Smith of the conversation (which we must, of course, then do).

Telephonitis

Some of us find the opportunity to gossip, or even to go on indefinitely about business, irresistible on a telephone. Why this should be, no one really knows, but it is a sad fact of business life. One of the worst known fates is to share an office with a colleague who suffers from this dreadful affliction. As with many of the worst diseases blighting the human condition, there is no known cure. Hints are invariably useless, and the only hope is ear muffs or a large hammer.

Confirm it

A couple of decades ago, it was common to require all important communications to be made, or at the least confirmed, in writing. Today, this is far less rigidly observed. It does remain good practice, however, when any agreement is made during a discussion (at a face-to-face meeting, as well as on the phone). The danger of misunderstanding, forgetfulness or even deliberate deceit will never, sadly, go away.

Some customers may find the need to confirm an order bothersome, and it is often sensible to take the initiative, and offer to confirm your understanding to him. As a safeguard in doing this, the name and position of the caller (if not previously known to us) should be established, and if possible a reference or order number.

Don't leave it hanging

It is essential to explain and get agreement before leaving the phone to seek a file, speak to another extension, transfer the call, or consult a colleague. It may be better to suggest abandoning a call and ringing back with information that is not to hand. If we arrange to ring back, we will need to check he is likely to be available, ensure we have the number he's at (which is not always the usual one), and *keep our promise.*

Don't use a hand
Consultations with colleagues while the hand covers the telephone are a long-established practice, but one that should be put to sleep for ever.

Just as those afflicted with deafness are particularly sensitive about conversations they cannot hear, so all of us readily believe plots are being hatched and insulting comments made behind someone else's hand. Besides, a hand in front of a telephone is a completely insecure device. If something cannot be said or asked with the telephone open, we should wait until the call has finished.

The telephone answering machine

These machines can help most organisations and are increasingly used by individuals, both at home and at work. However, like all pieces of equipment are worse than useless if mishandled.

The most common failing is not to check messages regularly and promptly, or to fail to ensure they are quickly and accurately passed on.

The wording, sound quality and diction of the recorded messages may be so stilted or so inaudible as to positively dissuade customers from trusting their needs to the machine.

Checking

I once had a boss who would ring his office, every so often, in what he thought was a disguised voice. No one was ever quite sure of his motives for this, but we presumed he was checking how telephone callers were dealt with. If this was so, his practice was quite a good one, although maybe a thinly disguised voice was not the best way of doing it.

Customers will on occasion complain about telephone problems, but there is no real substitute for experiencing them at first hand. Asking a wife or reliable friend to make occasional check calls is one way of finding out. Long-standing customers whose loyalty is unquestioned may help in the same way. It may even be possible to introduce a lighter or competitive note by inviting all staff to make such calls once in a while and see who are spotted

before announcing themselves. It is important that whatever
method is adopted staff do not feel they are being spied on.

Thought-starters

1. What proportion of your organisation's customer-contact is
   by means of the telephone?
2. Does your telephone equipment meet the needs of your
   organisation? If not, how does it fail? Have you recently
   examined what equipment is available that might help?
3. Do you have a peak problem for telephone calls? If so, when
   is it, and is there any action that might alleviate it?
4. Have telephone users in your organisation been trained
   (a) technically, or (b) in using skills?
5. Do you meet problems with over-protective secretaries in
   your work? If so, how do you overcome them? Does your
   secretary over-protect you?
6. Do you have problems with phone calls when you are out of
   your office? If so, why, and can you devise any solution?

Action points

1. Review telephone equipment and ensure the most suitable is
   installed (pages 96-7).
2. Consider automatic diversion of calls to meet problems of
   peak demand (page 97).
3. Review telephonists' job structures to relieve undue pressure
   (pages 97-8).
4. Provide internal telephone directories to regular customers
   (page 106).
5. Upgrade your own telephone skills and those of your staff
   (pages 99-111).

9
COMPLAINTS AND COMPLIMENTS

COMPLAINTS ARE a good thing, and should be treasured like gold. Just as adults must learn how to take and benefit from criticism, so organisations need to learn how to benefit from complaints. But just as many individuals find this a hard lesson to learn, so do many organisations and the staff in them.

Compliments are like gold too, if only because they are, for most of us, just as rare. Like complaints, they offer feedback which can help us improve our customer service, but usually with less power and value.

Complaints

Of course, no organisation wishes to receive too many complaints. But equally, any organisation that believes it can satisfy all of its customers all of the time is deceiving itself. If we receive no complaints, it is most unlikely to be because our service is perfect. More likely is that our customers believe, for whatever reason, that complaining is useless and are taking their custom elsewhere. Complaints offer the organisation the opportunity to put things right.

Every complaint an opportunity
Every complaint is an opportunity in several ways:

- *To avoid the harm caused by dissatisfied customers.* Loss of sales will result from a customer who does not complain or whose complaint is not well handled. This will be direct, from the loss of his business, and indirect from loss of the business of those he will tell of his dissatisfaction. Loss of sales may not be the only harm that dissatisfied customers do; some may, consciously or unconsciously, take revenge in other ways, or insist on extra attention and additional checks.

● *To improve operations for the future,* by swift remedial and preventive action, thus improving the overall appeal of its services.

● *To supplement, on a continuing basis, the market information it may get in other ways.*

● *To learn what is important to a particular customer.*

● *To increase the brand loyalty of the complainant.* A well-handled complaint frequently has the effect of binding the customer to the organisation and its product or service closer than before. This can happen because of the opening it gives for building a direct relationship with the complainant, and the chance to demonstrate efficiency and individual care in rectifying the cause of trouble.

These benefits are available whether we receive complaints from individual or organisational customers.

The key to obtaining these benefits is in the way we deal with complaints.

To handle complaints effectively, we need:

● A complaints policy
● Organisation structure
● Handling procedures
● Trained and effective staff and customers

If we lack many of these elements, then complaints may be a bad thing; complainants whose complaint is not well dealt with are the unhappiest customers of all.

Complaints policy

Policy and procedures are best committed to writing, so that they can be communicated to everyone. The document embodying the complaints policy should be well known to both staff and custom-ers. It should be published in sales literature, may be displayed on notices, and should be part of the training of all staff.

The policy should be helpful and not bureaucratic. As with other policies (see Chapter 11) it may be expressed in a brief, crisp statement:

'This company and its employees welcome complaints, and are committed to ensuring that every complaint will be received courteously, investigated as thoroughly as necessary, and acted on swiftly and appropriately.'

or more comprehensively:

'This organisation welcomes complaints as an aid to meeting its customers' needs even better. We will ensure:

— All staff are prepared to receive complaints, whether presented personally, in writing or by telephone. They will listen courteously, record faithfully, and initiate appropriate action immediately.
— Below the levels laid down in our procedure, immediate restitution will be offered. Above those levels, the complaint will be thoroughly and quickly investigated and answer given to the complainant as soon as possible.
— All complaints will be recorded and analysed so that the necessary action can be taken to avoid recurrence, and to ensure that our goods and services meet our customers' needs even more closely in the future.'

Organisation
Most organisations feel the need of one central department to which, at some stage, all complaints must be channelled.

The advantages of this are that it enables the laid-down procedures to be monitored, ensures that action is progressed, provides a basis of expertise and advice, is a natural centre for communication between the various departments or people involved, and acts as a facility for the gathering and analysis of information.

There may be two problems to be resolved in setting up and operating a complaints department; what are the boundaries of its action? and where does it fit into the total organisation structure?

Most authorities agree that over-centralisation does not work well. Flexibility and the needs for personal contact with complainants and the quickest possible action all suggest that maximum authority should be delegated to local staff. Except in the case of the very largest organisations (perhaps supermarket chains), this implies staff who are not actually members of a complaints department. The extent of the delegated authority, and the way complaints must be recorded, investigated and reported to the complaints department, will need to be spelt out clearly.

The place of the complaints department in the total organisation structure varies enormously and will depend to some extent on the nature of the organisation. Some organisations may place it within the manufacturing or laboratory areas, on the ground that most of their complaints refer to product quality. Others may place it within marketing or sales areas, on the basis that they have most direct contact with customers. If the organisation has a separate customer service department, this will form the natural home for the complaints department.

Wherever it is located, the real need is for sufficient authority to carry conviction with the heads of other major functions, and sufficient breadth of knowledge to handle complaints of all types. Without these, many of the potential lessons of complaints will not be learnt.

The title of the department is important. Many organisations feel that 'complaints department' acknowledges the receipt of frequent complaints, and also has a somewhat negative and forbidding ring to it. A common alternative is 'customer service', although this may be faulted on the grounds that it implies we only serve customers who complain. Also, if the view of customer service suggested in this book is accepted, it will be seen as a far wider activity than complaints handling. However, complaints handling will always be one aspect of this activity, and therefore always covered by the title.

Organisations will want to consider the best usage for their own situation; in order to avoid possible confusion with the wider function, the title 'complaints department' will be used in this chapter, but this is not intended to suggest it is necessarily the best choice.

Handling procedures

The procedures will need to cover complaints being received in writing, face to face, or by telephone. They must cover aspects such as:

- *To whom complaints should be directed,* bearing in mind the possible variations in circumstances, subject matter and seriousness. Good procedures usually give maximum discretion to local staff and minimise the need for reference to a 'head office' or another location.

● *What information must be obtained* from the complainant in order to progress a complaint. The most fundamental questions must always be to establish whether we are, in fact, the supplier. The amount of information needed will vary depending on the potential seriousness of the complaint.

● *What records must be made of a complaint,* and who must receive these records at the time and subsequently. Well-designed paperwork can help, even in the initial phase of a complaint, by providing a detached and methodical framework to what may be a heated discussion. Excessive paperwork, however, becomes annoying red tape (see Figure 6).

● *How to classify the seriousness of a complaint.* There are likely to be four classifications:

  – complaints which may be very serious
  – intermediate complaints
  – minor complaints which can be dealt with immediately at local level
  – complaints which are general in nature, and not tied to a specific transaction

● *How to identify and route very serious complaints.* All staff should have guidance on picking out immediately those complaints which may be particularly serious, and on the action they must then take. These complaints will usually be those which involve (or may involve):

  Personal injury
  Breach of the law
  Financial implications above a certain level.

Staff will need to have precise instructions on what to say (and not to say) to the complainant, what emergency action to take, and who to tell within the organisation.

● *What actions should be taken to investigate intermediate complaints.* This may be in the hands of a complaints department, who will progress the necessary investigations

Customer complaint

Date received:	Received by:
How received: Caller ☐ Telephone ☐ Letter ☐ (attach copy)	
Name of complainant	
Company name	

Company address		Telephone number (inc STD code and ext)

Goods complained of (if any)		Value

Proof of purchase	Were goods produced/returned?

Date:	Document:	Number:

Nature of complaint

Category of complaint: A ☐   B ☐   C ☐   D ☐

Immediate action taken	
Further action required	

Figure 6. *Example of a customer complaint form*

and ensure a full and appropriate reply is given. Where a complaint is proved (and in other cases where commercial considerations are judged to require an *ex gratia* settlement), options may include automatic full refund, full or partial refund after investigation, replacement, repair, compensation, apology, disciplinary action against staff, customer advice or training. It is important to realise and accept the difference in customer eyes between refund and the issue of a credit note. Legal considerations apart, the former is vastly more satisfying than the latter, which conveys the feeling of sharp practice by tying the wronged customer to a further purchase.

● *How to handle minor complaints.* There is overwhelming evidence that speed of handling complaints is of the utmost importance in retaining customer goodwill. To provide the speediest solution and minimise the costs of investigation, many organisations give authority for automatic refunds or other suitable settlement to appropriate local staff up to a certain value or within other criteria.

● *General complaints.* Some complaints may not be about a specific transaction, but about some general aspect of the organisation or its image. They may refer, for example, to long-term policies, or very general matters such as the livery of vehicles. In some cases, such complaints carry suggestions about possible improvements. These may not always be taken very seriously. It is true that some may be the result of rather superficial thinking, occasionally produced by someone with a bee in his bonnet. On the other hand, many are produced as the result of genuine interest, and represent a real opportunity to create customer goodwill.

● *The action to be taken when complaints are rejected.* Something must be done; they can never be left hanging in the hope they will go away. Once again, speed of response is vital. Even this stage, if properly handled, they may offer two opportunities to create goodwill. A swift, courteous and reasoned rejection may actually do more good than a grudging and dilatory acceptance. (By the same token, clumsy rejection can be a potent source of further complaint.)

If the problem has been caused by some fault on the part of the customer we may, rather than heaping guilt on him, gain goodwill by helping him to sort out the mess. The customer who has misread a specification, or misunderstood his own needs, can be made ours for life if we (a) set out to minimise his embarrassment, and (b) offer him positive, skilful assistance in his hour of need.

● *What use is made of complaint records.* The records can provide a goldmine of information about how our service is perceived by customers. They should be exploited to the full by regular study. The study will probably be of two kinds.

First, immediate case-by-case examination by someone with sufficient experience to decide which may indicate failures which might recur or are symptomatic of something deeper.

Second, later statistical analysis to establish whether complaints indicate any significant trends that suggest long-term problems with products, processes or personnel. In both cases, there should also be sufficient authority to ensure that the other departments or individuals involved take necessary action.

The personal factor
Perhaps the biggest obstacle to obtaining these advantages is the feeling of guilt and the defensive reactions which complaints can so easily generate in the employees handling them. To be on the receiving end of a complaint may tax our interpersonal skills to or beyond their limit.

Two sources of help are available: correct selection of staff, and good training. Beyond noting its importance, staff selection is outside the scope of this book. Training is now examined.

Four groups need training; all staff, front-line staff, complaints specialists, and customers.

All staff, whatever their job, should be made aware of the complaints policy and procedures during induction to the organisation. But they should also be reminded of it in appropriate ways, perhaps by reference during other training, perhaps by suitably displayed posters, perhaps by occasional brief seminars. Each individual should be clear at all times what action he should take and what he should not do if he is on the receiving end of a complaint. Supervisors should check and support their staff to ensure this happens.

Front-line staff, who have regular customer contact, will have received the basic briefing in the same way as all other staff. Beyond this, they will need to know the complaints handling procedures in more detail.

In addition, they will need to have undergone training designed to help them cope with the psychological pressures of handling complaints face to face, by telephone or letter.

To be effective, such training is likely to last at least one day initially, and will need boosting by additional brief sessions at intervals at which staff can discuss experiences, successes and problems in an unthreatening atmosphere. There are a number of proven techniques available including role-playing exercises, the use of closed-circuit television and some of the excellent films available covering this area.

Complaints specialists will have received training given to all and to front-line staff. In many cases, they may have been selected from those who have had experience in these areas.

In addition, they must be the experts in every aspect of the organisational procedure, knowing the authority they and others can exercise in varying circumstances. They must be familiar with documentation and its use.

They will need to know about the function and powers of the various consumer protection organisations and how these may relate to specific areas of complaint their organisation might experience.

They should have good knowledge of the law applying to consumer matters in their organisational field; sale of goods, description and labelling of goods, contract, direct and indirect liability etc.

It is likely that a much higher proportion of complaints will reach them in written form. They will benefit from training in effective letter writing, and should be supported by a series of appropriate standard letters covering common situations.

Customers. Many customers are highly nervous about complaining.

If, however, we accept that complaints are (in reasonable numbers) to be encouraged, we will gain by giving customers more help in complaining. If they have been given guidance, it is likely that their complaints will be made with less emotion and personal animosity, and they will feel that the organisation expects and welcomes their action. They will have the skill to pinpoint what has gone wrong more quickly and accurately, thus saving us time and effort.

Large organisations, trade associations or government agencies may see benefit in producing comprehensive guides to complaining. Smaller organisations may consider incorporating advice on complaints into other literature, in poster form or in simple give-away leaflets. Some hotel and restaurant chains offer guidance on complaints on their menus, receipts or other paperwork. Packing slips enclosed with goods may indicate how to initiate a complaint. Statutory bodies such as Transport Users Consultative Committees produce posters and leaflets explaining how to complain in the area for which they are responsible.

'Comments Boxes' may be used to invite complaints. By offering the option of anonymous comment, they may encourage more customers to give us feedback, both positive and negative.

Objection may sometimes be raised on the basis that such actions suggest to customers that the organisation gives a bad service; in fact, the suggestion conveyed is that the organisation is keen to give the best possible service. Occasionally staff may feel that such an invitation insults their capabilities; in fact, it helps to protect them by releasing the tensions in customers who are unhappy but unsure how to act. A final objection may be that it will increase the volume of complaints. This is true, and is (within very broad limits) exactly what we want.

Some do's and don'ts of face-to-face complaint-handling

Do:

- Allow time for the complainant to release his annoyance by an initial period of active listening; allow him to 'let off steam'.
- Check tactfully at an early stage that the product was, in fact, supplied by your organisation.
- Remember that every employee represents the whole organisation as far as the customer is concerned; don't

pass the buck because you were not involved in the subject matter of the complaint.

- Take any appropriate steps to make the complainant physically comfortable and relaxed; invite him into an office, to sit down, to have coffee or tea etc, depending on circumstances.
- Demonstrate genuine concern and a desire to help the complainant to solve the problem at every stage.
- Help the complainant to express his complaint, asking tactful but structured questions to elicit the relevant facts and clear away irrelevancies.
- Depending on the relevant organisational procedures, either make a record of the complaint, offer appropriate action, or refer the complainant to the person who can help.
- In every case, ensure that at the end the complainant knows exactly what subsequent action will be taken and by whom.

Don't:

- Allow feelings of personal guilt or anger either towards the complainant or towards the wrong he may have suffered to affect your response.
- Argue or try to score off the complainant verbally, even if an opportunity occurs.
- Express any view about the actions of other individuals or the organisation as a whole.
- Handle a serious complaint about yourself beyond the initial phase; involve a suitable senior colleague as soon as possible.
- 'Cause jump' or allow the complainant to force a particular interpretation on the situation without adequate evidence.
- Make any statement that can be construed as an acceptance of liability for any error.
- Assume the complainant is a trouble maker or that his complaint is trivial.
- Accept delay from any cause within your control.

Compliments

It is great to be complimented on the service we provide; sadly compliments are and always will be fewer and less important than complaints.

This is principally because of what may be called, in memory of Sherlock Holmes, the 'dog that didn't bark in the night' syndrome (see the story *Silver Blaze*). Things that go wrong are noticed; things that do not go wrong are usually unnoticed.

Of course, in many ways this is entirely fair. If we set out to give a good service and succeed, there is really nothing to comment on, unless we have had to cope with quite unusual difficulties (storm, fire, earthquake, etc). But there are two practical effects; we cannot rely on compliments to give much meaningful feedback on our performance and the needs of our customers, and we must take steps to remind customers in appropriate ways of all the things we do right. It is a task for our public relations or marketing departments (if we have them—if not, for us) to ensure that the public are gently reminded of our successes, both the regular, continuing ones and the occasional spectacular ones.

Sadly, many of the compliments that *are* received prove to have an ulterior motive. Often, they are nothing more than a gentle and polite introduction to a complaint. Other hidden agendas might include requests for free samples or other favours such as donations, sponsorship, research information or company literature for the careers room. It may, of course, be a sound commercial (or moral) decision to agree to some of these requests.

Some organisations handle compliments in the public affairs department, if they have one. A complaints department provides a natural point for handling compliments, as it will already have the necessary channels of internal communication, and can incorporate the feedback from compliments with its analysis of complaints to give a more comprehensive picture. In corresponding with the public, however, it must make sure it uses different headed paper and job titles!

One of the most important aspects of compliment handling is to ensure that they are channelled to the staff involved. We all work harder and better for knowing that we are appreciated.

Thought-starters

1. Consider occasions on which you have complained as a customer, both on behalf of your organisation and as an individual. On which occasions in each category was the response most and least satisfactory? What was your

reaction to the unsatisfactory reactions: did you buy again, stop buying, or what?

2. Has your organisation a complaints policy and procedure? If so, do they work well, and how might they be improved? If not, try drafting an outline.

3. What are the commonest sources of complaint about your organisation's service? How do you know? What action has been or should be taken?

4. Does your organisation receive compliments? If so, what about? Are they justified? What happens to them?

Action points

1. Agree and publish widely a complaints policy (pages 113-14).

2. Give clear complaints settlement authority to local staff (pages 114-15).

3. Establish categorisation of complaints by seriousness and link to clear handling procedures (pages 116-19).

4. Analyse complaint records to discover action points (page 119).

5. Provide published guidance for customers on how to complain (pages 120-21).

6. Provide 'comments boxes' for customers' comments (page 121).

7. Upgrade your own complaint handling skills and those of your staff (pages 119-22).

10
BETTER HARDWARE

BY HARDWARE IS meant the environment, buildings, equipment and other physical objects involved in the service of customers and potential customers. These may include:

Car parks
Yards, gardens, etc
The outside of buildings
The inside of buildings
Telephone equipment
Notices, posters and signs
Public address systems
Counters, booking windows and furniture
Equipment and machinery
Vehicles
Security devices
Staff uniforms, dress, etc
Product aspects

Not every organisation has customer service that is affected by all these factors, but for those that have, the effect may be considerable. In each case, the need is to view the facilities through customers' eyes; to see the familiar as if it was unfamiliar.

Car parks

Car parks have an importance in customer relations quite out of proportion to their functional role. Shoppers with a choice of several towns, for example, often choose by the car parking at least as much as by the shops themselves.

Parking is not only important in the retail trade; hotels, restaurants, and railway stations with inadequate parking suffer particularly, and so may any organisation with badly served offices that must be visited frequently by customers.

Many aspects affect customer reaction. How much space is there, and how likely is it to be free? How easy is it to find, both for drivers and pedestrians? How far is it from the building, and is the route exposed to the weather? If payment is required, what is the fee? Is the method of payment convenient? Are there reserved spaces for staff, and if so, are they marked clearly? What happens to the visitor who uses them? If there is provision for visitors, is it adequately policed, or filled up every morning by staff cars? Do visitors need car badges or stickers, and if so how do they get them? Are times of access limited, and if so, are they clearly indicated, and what happens if you are late? Is the car park staffed, and if so, are the staff courteous?

Surface car parks are greatly preferred to multi-storey parks, especially by women; multi-storey parks are felt to be dark and remote, especially at night, and entering by car, driving up steep ramps and round sharp bends, and parking in a confined space against what may be a continuous stream of cars, is unpopular.

The carless

While in this subject area, it is worth remembering that there will never be such a thing as a fully motorised society. About a third of the population do not and never will arrive by car. The old, disabled and infirm, the young, the uninsurable, those who hate driving, those who cannot afford a car and those who simply do not have the use of one, will always remain. Any customer-contact organisation that forgets this in its planning will suffer.

Yards and gardens

In some businesses, yards can be dirty, confusing and dangerous places. The combination of visitors on foot and in cars, delivery vehicles, fork-lift trucks, stock, pallets and waste can be lethal, metaphorically and occasionally literally. They need to be seen through customer eyes, rather than the eyes of those to whom they are a comfortable, familiar midden.

The organisation lucky enough to possess a garden to which

customers have access has a major asset. If more business was done in gardens, the world would be a better place.

The outside of buildings

Parkinson (*Parkinson's Law*[1]) challenges the traditional view about buildings, suggesting with a devastating mixture of levity and clarity that if an investor had to choose between an organisation housed in a splendid modern building replete with every conceivable convenience, and one operating from Nissen huts in the muddy back garden of a Victorian terraced house, he would be wise to choose the latter. The second organisation, he suggests, is more likely to be at the start of a phase of dynamic growth, whilst the first may well have grown to the point of exhaustion, or 'ingelilitis'.

The traditional view of buildings, however, sees them as symbols of the stability and prosperity of the organisation. Sadly, this is likely to be the view of our customers. Buildings invariably convey a message about the organisation that uses them. The image created may be of wealth and opulence, economic leanness, solidarity, civic pride, commercial virility, traditional values, progressiveness, or whatever. But the message may not be what we intend. In particular, if the building is rented, or in multiple occupation, it may give the wrong message.

Government departments suffer a particular problem. Because they spend public money, they must not be seen to be spending wastefully. This probably commands the agreement of all taxpayers except those who actually have to use the poverty-stricken and inadequate facilities that may thus be provided for the department's customers.

If we work in a building, we take its external appearance for granted. While most organisations are reasonably effective in their housekeeping, and will arrange painting and the replacement of broken windows, they do not always review the visual image as a whole with a customer eye. How many shopkeepers clutter their windows with a plethora of posters advertising special offers? How many offices appear dull and forbidding, when a little well-used paint or a few simple changes could work wonders?

The inside of buildings

The door
The interior problems of many buildings start in trying to get there. Larger retailers have mostly realised how important is the design of doors, some going to the lengths of completely eliminating them and substituting a curtain of welcoming warm air. Other organisations have not.

The proportion of customers lost because the door they pushed was locked, with no visible indication or obvious reason, will probably never be known. But to these must be added customers lost through trying to push the revolving door the wrong way round, and those afflicted by shyness who, faced with a solid panel, turn away unsure of their welcome. Perhaps this total is still small, but a much bigger number of those who do finally get into the building will be tense, annoyed and measurably less inclined to buy.

Reception
'Welcome' on the mat is good for customer relations, but those without a mat need something else. Most organisations have given thought to and spent money on their reception area, but not always with success, if only because styles change so rapidly. Also, impressiveness cannot make up for lack of the right facilities. Which desk do I go to? Where do I wait? Where is the loo? Why is it so draughty, noisy and full of people dashing from side to side and back and forth? Where, above all, is the warmth of welcome?

Privacy
'Good Lord,' cried the doctor's receptionist, as a patient booked in at the crowded surgery, 'here's the man with Aids'. That night, the patient's house was burnt down. Luckily, such extremes are rare, but lack of privacy for customers where it is needed is not. Not only medical reception facilities, but the public areas of banks, building societies, tax and social security offices often lack such provision.

Seeing each other
A good layout should allow the customer to be in full view of the staff he needs to deal with, and *the staff of the customer*. If a customer walks into a shop, reception area, waiting room or office in which no staff who can help him are visible something is wrong.

The jolly extrovert will call out 'Shop!' in a loud and jolly voice; the rest of us will wait around uncertainly, trying the effect of a cough, possibly tapping a counter tentatively, and in the end, if no one appears, walking out. An old-fashioned brass bell may work wonders for customer relations.

Customers also feel tense if staff need to disappear during a transaction; good layout should avoid this.

Expert errors
Architects and other experts can easily miss important factors. Airports where no enquiry desk is provided within the transit area seem a clear example. The design of buildings to which large numbers of customers have access, such as supermarkets, hospitals, hotels, colleges, libraries and passenger terminals should be customer-driven. We may need to remind ourselves that the need to service its customers is the reason the building exists. The cynical layman occasionally gets the feeling that few architectural awards are given for utility and convenience.

General ambience
Passages, staircases, and lifts produce a frame of mind in the customer before he starts to talk business. Is this frame of mind the one we want? To position in a far corner of the site offices or showrooms to which customers often go is asking for problems. Noise level is far more apparent to a visitor than to those working in a building; it may be a particular problem if transactions have to be conducted from an outer, noisy area to an inner, quieter one, as in a booking hall or theatre foyer. Lighting, both natural and artificial, can set the whole tone and feeling of a building, as well as affecting convenience and safety.

The disabled
Disabled people are now more frequently catered for in the design of buildings, but there remains a lot to do.

Keep the party clean
Of course, cleanliness and tidiness are important, but it is easy to overlook a clutter of files on a window sill or an untidy desk that one lives with every day.

Telephone equipment

Telephone equipment has a bigger effect on the customer service of some organisations than any other piece of hardware. For them, this is the gate through which most customers establish and maintain contact.

Delays in answering, poor sound quality, lost calls, problems in transferring calls, and crossed lines can be death to business. The annoyance, frustration and misunderstanding that unsuitable equipment can cause, and the volume of business it may lose or never obtain as a result is incalculable. It is easy to fall behind. Technology in this field is continually advancing, and each generation of equipment offers more that may help our customer relations. Do we know what is currently available?

Direct lines for those who have extensive customer contact will eliminate delay and ensure immediate connection with the right person or department; the investment may be very cost-effective.

Telephone answering machines may help when customers need to make contact while we are away. Automatic transfer of calls may be even better in some circumstances. Machines can also be used to filter out undesirable calls, if we have a special problem in this way.

Notices, posters and signs

Signs of all kinds can be a problem. Some of the commonest difficulties are:

Missing sign
Ludicrously simple, this is also ludicrously common.

Lack of continuity
Strictly speaking, this is just a special case of the missing sign, but it is so common that it justifies special mention. One sign directs us down a corridor, for example, but at the next problem point, as often as not a T-junction, we find none. To signpost every junction may be tedious, costly or unsightly, but to do anything less negates the whole process.

Ambiguity
'Stop while the red light flashes' said the sign at the railway level

crossing, blissfully unaware that in some parts of Britain 'while' means 'until' (as in 'I'll be here while five o'clock').

Notices at the ends of station platforms have a habit of not saying what they mean—'Passengers must cross the line by the footbridge' may raise questions such as 'Why, if I'm already on the correct platform?' or 'What if I'm only here to meet a friend?' But to be fair, most people grasp the message.

The commonest cause of ambiguity is positioning. From here, the arrow seems to point this way, but if we stand over there, maybe it could seem to point that...

No help for the damned
What if we do wander off the yellow brick road? How are we going to get back? It is unreasonable to expect signs that cover every possibility from every angle, but some help should be available, especially in difficult areas. Some hospitals can be particularly good at this, displaying multiple signs at every corridor or pathway junction.

Bad positioning
Signs describing street parking restrictions are often unreadable or invisible to motorists in their cars desperately trying to park. Ignorance of the law is no excuse, but for those of us without this support, it is not enough to answer; 'But there is a sign there', if the sign cannot easily be read.

Too small, too large, wrong colour, wrong style
Most airport and station signs are now produced in a well-designed, standard format that communicates their function immediately. But not every business has got these factors right.

Too many signs
Few things are more confusing and counter-productive than a clutter of too many, unco-ordinated signs.

Impolite signs
At least one local authority words the signs in its parks 'Keep off the grass'. It would be interesting to know whether this wording was more or less effective than signs using the short additional word 'Please'.

Misleading signs

A provincial theatre in the Midlands for many years had a
large sign suspended from the ceiling of the foyer, above the
point where soft drinks are sold in the interval, reading 'Ice
cream'. Ice cream is not sold at this point, even to those who
may have queued for 15 minutes under the impression that it
was, nor are the staff particularly polite to such individuals,
indicating that no one in their right mind could make such an
obvious error. The reason for this situation, which does not
appear to bother the theatre management, has never been
made clear.

In the days of trading stamps, many a motorist bought petrol at
a garage whose sign offered 'Quad stamps' only to be told when
paying the bill that 'they had run out'. Few motorists, as the garages involved knew well, would go to the trouble of invoking the
majesty of the law for stamps worth a few pence.

Experienced motorists also know that the chances of roadworks
actually following a sign saying 'Roadworks' or a hazard following
a pair of flashing yellow lights on a motorway are no better than
two out of three.

The public address system

Few aspects of customer service generate more complaints than
the Tannoy or public address system.

A PA system can only operate as a supplement to other means.
Chaos would rapidly descend on an airport or station where passengers had to rely only on the PA, without arrival or departure
boards or staff at hand.

PA is a useful aid for:

- Giving emergency instructions
- Giving up-to-the-minute information on changing
  situations
- Supplementing other sources of information (such as
  notices) or drawing attention to them
- Creating a more attractive environment (ie by playing
  suitable music)
- Selling products or services

Common problems in use include:

- Speech too fast, too slow, or lacking clarity

- Poor tone, conveying aggression, lack of confidence, or anxiety
- Bad timing; announcements either too early, too late, or coinciding with other noise or distractions
- Bad wording, causing ambiguity or uncertainty
- Use too rare or unreliable, leading to lack of reliance by the customer
- Use too frequent, especially with repetition, leading to rejection by the customer as redundant or irritant

Good training and scripting can do a lot to help.

Some organisations use pre-recorded announcements covering many situations, to ensure that the best possible standards of wording and diction are maintained. These may be legitimate, but have their drawbacks, especially if used to cover emergency applications. Pressing the wrong button can have shattering effects, as the passengers on a British Airways flight found out when they were cruising slumberously at 35,000 feet over the Bay of Biscay. They were (according to press reports) told on the PA that their plane would be making an emergency landing in the sea in a few moments, that they must don their lifejackets immediately and await the Captain's further instructions. There were no doubt some trenchant comments about pre-recorded announcements on their subsequent normal touchdown at Heathrow.

Playing music through the PA system can upset some customers or have other unexpected effects. Research is needed before going too far.

Counters, booking windows and furniture

The forbidding effect of being required to transact business through tiny windows or grilles has been generally realised. Unfortunately, the needs of security make such barriers very difficult to do without. However, some of the most recently designed bank branches are designed in a way which allows staff and customers to meet and talk in natural, relaxed proximity whilst making the robber's job near-impossible. A similar approach may help in other situations.

Furniture has a strong effect on the atmosphere in which business is done. The classic error is to create a psychological barrier between supplier and customer (or client, as more often in this case). Some doctors, solicitors and salespeople may learn here from personnel officers, of whom the more enlightened long ago stopped interviewing from behind a desk with the light shining in the victim's eyes.

Equipment and machinery

Equipment and machinery may affect customer relations in several ways.

Some machinery has a direct effect on customer service. How many of us have stood hesitantly in front of a slot machine, eyeing the chocolate we so much crave inside, weighing up the chances that we can successfully get at it, and what we should do if we can't? Cash, food and drink dispensing machines are in this category, but so are machines operated by staff when serving customers, such as credit card and ticket-issuing machines. If badly designed or faulty in operation, any of these can make life difficult for staff and customer alike.

Many a diner has chosen steak Diane for the simple pleasure of seeing it cooked. The opportunity to visit the flight deck of an aircraft was, before the days of the hijacker, a major pleasure for many airline customers. Some civil engineering contractors realised a couple of decades ago that the sight of good equipment skilfully used interests everyone. Farmers have discovered the strong customer attraction of seeing machinery and processes at work; some derive more income from the viewing galleries round the milking parlour (and the other revenue from the parties they attract) than from selling the milk.

We all enjoy watching others work. Our interest is greatest when real skill is involved; people will stand for hours craning over the shoulder of a painter or a potter, but it is still strong when the tasks are done entirely by machinery. Quite a few manufacturing operations might benefit from opening up at least part of their factory so that outsiders could see the process at work.

The sight of old-fashioned or badly maintained machinery or inefficient processes, on the other hand, will hardly inspire confidence.

Vehicles

Vehicles and their drivers affect customer relations.

The effect of freight vehicles spreads not only to customers of the organisation, but to the public at large.

The pollution caused by exhaust fumes and noise, the effect of vibration on buildings and spray from heavy vehicles all worry many people. Vehicles that are (or seem) too large for the job, creating obstruction on unsuitable roads or at customers' premises, may upset the customer. They may upset the customer's customers even more, if, for example, they cause problems in his car park or yard. To be trapped behind a slow or overloaded lorry (whether it is overloaded legally doesn't matter to the suffering motorist) will cause many customers or potential customers to curse the name painted on the vehicle. Dirty vehicles and those that create the impression of being badly maintained or inadequate for their job also harm the image of the organisation whose name they carry.

Driving standards and road manners matter enormously. The vehicle on the road and its driver are seen together as representatives of the organisation whose name they display. Driving in convoy is a particular problem; what seems an impressive symbol of market strength to the supplier and carrier may appear as a dangerous nuisance to other road users.

The design of passenger vehicles, whether taxis, buses, trains, aircraft or ships, is an important aspect of the primary service provided by passenger carriers, and is therefore outside the scope of this book. Dirt, maintenance standards, inappropriate size and pollution are aspects of customer service, and have the most direct impact.

The occasional extra touch can have a positive effect; 'Have a nice day' painted on the back, for example, or the bus blind that says not 'Depot only', but 'Sorry, I'm not in service'.

Security

Security needs can work in the opposite direction to the needs of customer service.

The horrors of air hijacking ensure that virtually all air passengers now see thorough security at airports as a welcome addition to customer service. But this is a special case.

To be stopped, questioned or even searched on one's way to negotiate for, buy or use something can be enough to stop the deal. Security at the entrance to a factory or office poses both behavioural and hardware problems. The trappings of quasi-military uniform, barriers, video cameras, X-ray machines, passes, security posts, bells, locks, badges and visitors' books do not convey a feeling of welcome to the customer.

It is worth challenging what is done to our customers in the name of security. What security is needed? What is being secured, and against what or whom? What consequences would flow from a breach of that security? Granted the need, is each element necessary, and is it being done in the best way, not only for security but for customer relations? Shop-lifting presents a major challenge to retailers, especially in view of recent suggestions that the bulk of stock loss may arise from staff rather than customers.

Staff uniforms and dress

Well-turned-out staff give a good image to any organisation.

However, clothing has a powerful influence on the wearer and his self-image and behaviour. The morale of a workforce can be enhanced or destroyed by its choice; even small details of design may have a surprisingly large effect. Uniforms, especially worn by males, tend to have military overtones which do not always match other customer service objectives. Careful consultation with both staff and customers can help a lot in this intimate area.

Product aspects

The product itself is by definition not part of customer service, but it may have service aspects.

The most important of these is that no amount of good customer service can support a bad primary product (or service) indefinitely.

Some would argue that bad design is a service failing, in the sense that all too many products perform their primary function adequately, but are awkward or unpleasant to use.

The quality of the product is also strongly linked in many minds to customer service, although this is not an aspect of service as we have defined it.

The stock holding of slow-moving products may have service implications. The natural reaction when a line sells very slowly is to eliminate it; but this will cause much inconvenience to the occasional buyer, who may be a frequent buyer of faster-moving lines. 'Service stock' may be a wise investment to meet such situations.

Thought-starters

1. When you have been a customer, have you been impressed by any oustanding examples of effective or counter-productive hardware? What was so bad or so good about them? Do they suggest any lessons for your own organisation?
2. What aspects of hardware are most important to the customer service given by your organisation?
3. Which of these aspects currently damage customer service, or fail to contribute to it as they might? In each case, why?
4. In each case, (a) what might be done to improve the level of service; (b) what would be the level of capital and running costs; (c) would the improvement be measurable financially or only indirect, and (d) would it be worth making?

Reference

1. *Parkinson's Law, or the Pursuit of Progress*, C Northcote Parkinson, John Murray

Action points

1. Review outside and inside all buildings from the angle of customer convenience and safety (pages 127-8).
2. Check the layout for necessary customer privacy and convenience of all transactions (page 128).
3. Install direct telephone lines for key customer-contact staff (page 130).
4. Check signs, notices, noise-level and furniture of all customer-contact areas from the customer's angle (pages 130-32, 133-4).
5. Check installation and use of PA equipment (page 132).
6. Check efficiency and suitability of all equipment and machinery used in customer service (pages 132-3).
7. Consider exposing processes or working machinery to customer view (page 134).
8. Review the customer impact of freight vehicle operations (pages 134-5).
9. Upgrade staff dress/uniforms (page 136).

PART 3

MANAGEMENT

11
POLICY AND ORGANISATION

IN THIS CHAPTER, we will see what contribution can be made to good customer service by setting policy and establishing a good structure for the organisation. Both may seem remote from the scene of action, but getting them right creates a strong foundation for success in the front line.

Policy

A carefully thought out, well written and accepted policy is the best foundation for effective long-term management action. It tells everyone where they are and in which direction they should be going.

Larger organisations usually accept the benefit a written policy offers; but even a one-person business can gain a lot from standing back, defining what its policy is, and committing it to paper. The discipline of producing a policy helps to sharpen perceptions and clarify views, whatever the size, and however many people are involved.

It is possible to be cynical about policy. One organisation may have a manual of fine, well-phrased policies but be in chaos. Another may make brilliant managerial decisions without a scrap of written policy. But such anomalies do not detract from the benefits that a good policy can offer.

A policy on customer service (as on other aspects of management) helps:

- Clear thinking about and thorough examination of the subject
- Effective communication with everyone concerned

141

- Consistency over time
- Consistency between the various departments or individuals concerned

Policy in any one area, such as customer service, must be consistent with overall organisational policy, and with policies in other areas. Policy conflict can do serious harm, and a conscious process of policy making should highlight conflicts between departmental or functional policies so that they can be resolved.

Top up or bottom down?
The actual process of policy making can yield benefits in staff relations. Conventionally, policy is made at the top and communicated down the management ladder. But it does not have to happen this way; policy can be made bottom-up.

Tapping the knowledge and creativity that exists at every level within an organisation is not easy. Suggestions schemes and briefing groups do something to release it, but in most organisations there is a lot more that could be done. 'The boss knows best' and 'I'm only paid to do as I'm told' are two sides of the same dull and valueless coin.

Bottom-up policy making begins with discussion in informal general meetings to which all staff or all staff in each area are invited. Senior staff should participate in these meetings, but leadership is usually best undertaken by someone outside the formal management structure, perhaps a trainer or consultant. Final decisions are still made at the top level, but if they vary from the conclusions of the meetings then the reasons for the changes should be clearly explained.

Bottom-up policy making does not by any means always work. To be invited for the first time to help make the policy within which one operates may even produce a feeling of insecurity. The process needs skilful handling, and will only succeed in some situations. But when it does, it will generate the satisfaction and commitment which comes from knowing we have contributed and been recognised for our contribution. The approach may be well worth experimenting with.

Writing a customer service policy statement
There is a danger of writing policy in self-conscious and fine-sounding language that means nothing. But good policy is never

long-winded, and effective statements are usually confined to things that actually need saying. Nothing is gained by cluttering them up with truisms and platitudes. On the other hand, they do need to be sufficiently comprehensive to take account of any situation that can reasonably be foreseen.

The policy must embody the main drive and intentions of the organisation in the area of customer service. It should answer the questions, 'How important are our customers to us?' and 'How exactly do we set about serving our customers?'

A short, simple customer service policy might read:

> To contribute to the profitability and long-term prosperity of the organisation by ensuring that concern for and interest in its customers are at the centre of every phase of its operations.

Other organisations may approach policy by a longer statement, possibly based on the main phases of customer service, and saying something about each of them that is relevant to their operations. Thus a manufacturer might have a customer service policy such as the following:

CUSTOMER SERVICE POLICY

Aim. It is the aim of the Company to know the needs of the customer and to treat them as of highest priority at all times.

Systems. Every system and procedure shall be designed and operated as far as practicable to meet the needs of the customer. The specific aims will include convenience and simplicity of use, accuracy, reliability, timeliness and compatibility with customers' systems.

Customer relationships. It must be the aim of every company employee, when in contact with customers and potential customers, to establish and maintain a positive, helpful and friendly relationship. Business must be conducted efficiently and speedily. Necessary information must be supplied at all stages, and particularly when problems of any sort have arisen or may arise.

Environment. All aspects of premises which are open to customers must be planned and maintained to ensure cleanliness, safety and convenience.

Complaints. Complaints from customers must be dealt with

helpfully, fairly and quickly. All must be recorded in the laid-down form, and evaluated according to the established departmental guidelines.

Published policy
Once written, a policy will need wide circulation. It can be published, so that, apart from its internal value, it can have a direct impact on customer relations: we have pinned our colours to the mast. Some organisations use customer service policy as a major part of their public relations activity, printing and circulating it in sales literature, catalogues and brochures, or posting it up for all to see in offices, showrooms or shops.

This can help by giving confidence to customers at the point of sale, and it acts as a reminder to staff. In the right circumstances, it may have a directly beneficial effect on sales, as well as on less tangible aspects of customer relations.

Perhaps the only danger is the risk of promising in a legally enforceable form something which cannot be done every time. At least this possibility should have the benefit of concentrating the minds of those who must write the policy.

Regular reviews
It is said that if a frog is placed in a beaker of water which is then slowly heated to boiling point, the poor creature has no nervous mechanism which will warn it of the steady rise in temperature, and will sit still until it is nicely cooked. This inability to detect slow, progressive change can afflict organisations, including some of the largest and most sophisticated.

Policy cannot be carved in tablets of stone. It will need reviewing at regular intervals, to check whether market conditions, technology and the other factors have changed sufficiently to call for changed policies.

Do's and don'ts of policy

Do:

- Have a policy
- Consult all involved in operating the policy
- Use simple, direct language
- Cover all likely situations

- Ensure company and all departmental policies match
- Write it down
- Circulate to everyone involved
- Consider publishing to customers
- Review and update regularly.

Don't:

- Use empty and pompous language
- Set aims that cannot be reached
- Be unnecessarily long-winded.

Organisation structure

Customer service faces one major problem: it is not, in most organisations, recognised as a function. Finance, manufacturing, R&D, marketing, personnel and the rest have a name and a recognised role. What they do and their relationship with what others do is understood, both within the organisation and outside. In many cases, the staff who perform the work may be physically located together, and even if not, they are likely to be under the control of one boss. In some cases, their expertise may be supported by external professional bodies.

Customer service is like management, and possibly some other activities, in that it is carried out by many different people, in many different ways, across the whole organisation. Even if there is a department with the title of customer service, it is likely to cover only a small part of the total activity.

From this initial cause spring many of the problems of achieving the best customer service. Unless the importance of customer service is reflected in and underpinned by a suitable organisational structure, it will never play its crucial role in achieving success. A customer-driven philosophy must be supported by the right organisation structure.

Organisation structure is often like Topsy; it has a tendency to just grow. Small enterprises have little need of structure; too much rigidity can be harmful in the early stages. However, the larger one grows, the more essential structure becomes. It is a wise enterprise that knows when it has reached the critical point in its growth and creates a clear structure at the moment when it is needed.

Organisation structures must also be flexible and capable of developing and changing. It is all too easy for them to atrophy, and cease to match current needs. Organisational changes may be needed because of changes in the market-place, changes in product or technology, growth or contraction of the business, changes in personnel, or policy changes. A realisation of the central importance of the customer might be just such a change.

A good organisation structure should help to ensure defined responsibility for every phase, reduction in the number of points of customer contact, and a flexible approach.

The customer has a right to know who is responsible for every aspect of a transaction in which he is involved; so do the organisation's staff. Staff cannot communicate more than they know themselves. Whether face to face, on the telephone or in correspondence, nothing upsets customers more, and with better reason, than the feeling that no one will accept responsibility for their problem. Good organisation structure is an essential part of the solution to this difficulty.

Every boundary, whether between countries or departments in an organisation, is a potential cause of tension. Boundaries in business may cause delay, misunderstanding, omission or duplication. Whether the tension is latent and harmless or the cause of warfare and violence depends on history, circumstances and the characters of those currently involved.

Boundaries of one sort or another exist in every organisation of any size, but they should be few, undefended and flexible. If they are not, customer service will suffer.

Where should responsibility for customer service be placed?
The best option is almost certain to be a director or senior executive reporting to the chief executive, with functional responsibility for all aspects of customer service. Whether this person is supported by a department will depend on the size and nature of the organisation. However, before adopting this approach, some problems need facing, and there are alternatives that may be worth considering.

Apart from the nomination of a senior executive, overall responsibility for customer service may be structured in several other ways. Some organisations:

● Nominate an existing department
● Give the chief executive or one of his personal staff responsibility

- Co-ordinate customer service through routine board or management committee meetings
- Establish an *ad hoc* committee of departmental heads
- Use an already existing Customer service department

Existing department. The choice of department usually lies between the marketing, sales or distribution departments. The service department may sometimes be considered, and some organisations place it within finance or production departments. Exceptionally, a case might even be made for the research and development or personnel departments to take this role. Which is chosen will depend on how the organisation trades, how many customers it has and how it contacts them.

When physical distribution of the finished product to customers is a major aspect of activity, the distribution or logistics department will probably be the prime candidate. This may be the best within many manufacturing organisations.

If customer contact is a matter of many face-to-face meetings, as in retailing, it may be felt that marketing or sales should have the leading role. In many organisations, marketing may be the obvious candidate, because of its close contact with and understanding of customers and potential customers, and its ability to gather and process market information. Occasionally, where regular staff training is essential for effective customer service, the personnel or training department may be a logical home.

Research in the US suggests that customer service departments can work well as part of marketing, sales or distribution, depending on the type of organisation, but rarely work well when attached to finance or production.

Perhaps surprisingly, the service department is unlikely to be a good candidate for overall control and co-ordination of customer services, as its after-sales interests will be concentrated in a narrow (albeit important) corner of the whole field.

The design and research and development departments may have direct involvement in service. Many customer service problems, particularly of faulty products or maintenance and after-sales service, are caused by bad design, or failure to manufacture to specification. Where this is a common cause of complaints, customer service may find a home in a technical department, possibly a laboratory. However, as with after-sales service, it would be unusual for such an arrangement to give the breadth of coverage good customer service requires.

The chief executive. For the chief executive (or chairman, managing director, or general manager) to take personal responsibility for co-ordinating and directing customer service usually works well in a small organisation. It reflects the importance of the subject, and offers the best chance of effective co-ordination.

Whether this arrangement is practicable in larger organisations must depend on the interests and skills of the chief executive and the nature of his formal and informal relationships with other managers. In the case of a large organisation, there may be a case for appointing a member of the chief executive's personal staff to hold the co-ordinating role on his behalf and with his authority.

Use of routine meetings. The use of routine board or management committee or similar meetings to co-ordinate and drive the customer service activity is unlikely to succeed by itself. Such bodies may be unduly liable to the 'squeaky wheel' syndrome: giving too much attention to those who shout loudest. Anecdotal evidence, particularly when related to direct contacts of the board or committee members, may be given undue weight, while the time and possibly the expertise to explore the underlying issues may not be available.

Ad hoc committee of departmental heads. This can work well in some circumstances. It provides a forum for communication and co-ordination without detracting from the authority of individual managers, so that problems, ideas and information can be discussed positively.

The danger, as with all regular meetings, is that the committee may in due course lose its momentum, sense of urgency and direction. It may become a meeting of the second and even of the third eleven, as departmental heads find other priorities. It may get bogged down or come to be dominated by one member. Sometimes, it may become a cosy dining club justifying a monthly trip to town.

Good, inspirational chairmanship during and between meetings can help such a group to achieve much.

Already existing customer service department. If a department with this title already exists, it may not always have responsibility for the whole customer service function; it may be responsible for

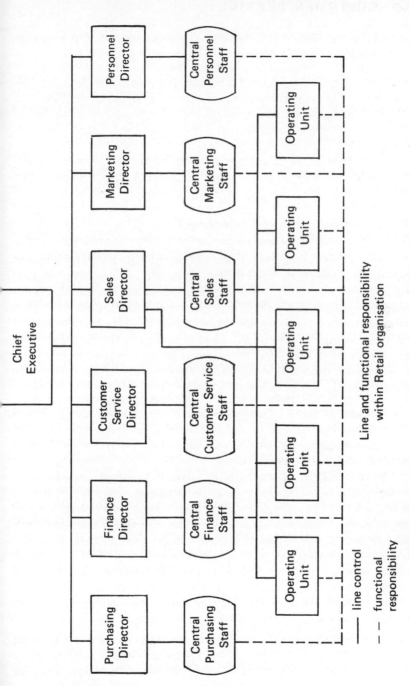

Figure 7. *Organisation structure for separate customer service department*

after-sales service, or for handling complaints only. Occasionally, this title may be given to the order-taking department.

Whether it is sensible to use such a department as the nucleus of a department with much wider responsibilities in the customer service area will depend on company politics, the personalities and skills of the various managers involved, the geographical distribution and nature of operations, possibly on industrial relations factors.

Establishment of a comprehensive customer service department may actually be easier when no department with that name already exists.

The new customer service department

The role of a comprehensive customer service department, if it is decided to establish one, will be twofold: its functional responsibilities and its departmental duties.

Functional responsibilities will include laying down policies and standards for the whole organisation, monitoring performance against these standards and initiating corrective action, raising awareness of the importance of good service, and co-ordinating action by other departments.

Departmental duties are likely to include handling serious complaints, maintaining and using complaints records, and possibly the control of after-sales service staff. The department may have its own survey staff, or may draw on the services of staff from the marketing department or outside specialists. Similarly, it may have its own training staff, or may use staff controlled by the personnel and training department.

The authority and responsibility given to the departmental head will make a big difference to the effectiveness of such a department. To work properly, he must rank at least on a par with other departmental heads, and have the same access to the chief executive or board. Only from this base will the department have any chance of carrying out its functional responsibilities.

The larger and more spread out an organisation is, the more important is the question of centralising or decentralising control of the customer service function. Many of the organisations with closest direct involvement in customer service have particularly wide geographical spread. These include chains of retail stores, hotels, cafés and restaurants, public transport undertakings, health, education and other government services.

For each of these, the question must be faced: to what extent should each unit be given authority to operate its own customer service policy, and to what extent should we insist that it works to standards and methods laid down and monitored centrally?

The authors of *The Winning Streak*,[1] talking about the general problem of centralised or decentralised decision-making, have no doubt: they speak of the need for 'deep-rooted decentralisation'. This view is widely held today. However, a railway could not function if each stationmaster could determine the width of the gauge; standards must inevitably be set centrally, even though maximum freedom to work within those standards may best be given to the local unit.

Thought-starters

1. Has your organisation a written policy? If so, what areas does it cover?
2. Has it a customer service policy? If so, do you know what it says?
3. Try drafting the ideal customer service policy for your organisation.
4. Which departments in your organisation have staff whose sole or main job is customer service?
5. Has your organisation any mechanism for central control or co-ordination of customer service activities and standards? If so, where is it, and does it work well; if not, where should it be?
6. Is the question of centralisation/decentralisation important to the success of customer service in your organisation? If so, which policy is followed now, does it work well, and how might it be improved?

Action points

1. Define and publish a customer service policy statement (pages 141-5).
2. Establish a director or senior executive reporting to the chief executive with full functional responsibility for all aspects of customer service (pages 146, 150-51).

Reference

1. *The Winning Streak*, Walter Goldsmith and David Clutterbuck, Weidenfeld and Nicolson, 1984

12
CUSTOMER-FRIENDLY SYSTEMS

A THOROUGH-GOING improvement of our standard of customer service cannot be achieved without looking closely at all the systems involved.

What is a system?

Anyone or any group of people who carry out a task repeatedly in the same way are using a system.

The task may be simplicity itself, like ringing up the price and placing the cash in the till, or it may have the complexity of a major stock-control system. It may be entirely manual, such as placing boxes of produce on a shelf in date order. It may use machinery or equipment, such as a ticket issuing machine or a fork-lift truck. It may be controlled personally, by the memory of the receptionist or the decision of the foreman in the loading bay. It may be controlled by a procedure on paper, such as the completion and filing of an application. It may be controlled automatically, such as a cash-dispensing machine.

No business of any size could be conducted entirely without systems, although the smallest organisations need very few, very simple systems. This is one of the many cogent reasons why small is beautiful. Perhaps an artist painting and selling masterpieces at irregular intervals may have no recognisable systems, but even he is likely today to need the help of someone such as an accountant to provide system back-up. In Britain, the last businesses operating without systems were probably eliminated by the onset of Value Added Tax.

Why systems may damage customer service

Systems are indespensable to business. They help, but they also have characteristic dangers, particularly in the field of customer service. The larger the organisation, the more danger it is in from its own systems.

The dangers of systems include:

- They are by nature inflexible, and may fail to respond to changed needs.
- They rarely cope well with extreme cases: the order which is very large or very small; unusual delivery constraints; the individualistic personality.
- They can all too easily be used as an excuse and a refuge for delays and errors.
- They may not match customer systems, especially electronic or mechanical systems.
- They may become an end in themselves, instead of a means to the end of greater all-round effectiveness.
- They may become involved in aspects of industrial relations which make them difficult to change or use effectively. 'Working to rule' is an example of this.
- They tend to inhibit, possibly even prohibit, creativity and innovation.

The attitude to systems should thus always be wary; they are good servants but bad masters. Once an organisation can be called a bureaucracy, it has become an automaton—a corpse under the control of the systems of its own creation. Our systems will be a key area affecting our customer service performance, and any attempt to improve this must include a very hard look at them, especially those directly involving customers.

Customer service systems

While any system may have an effect on customer service, some have direct impact from their very nature. They include:

- Sales/ordering systems
- Supply/logistics systems
- Accounting/payment systems
- After-sales service systems

- Complaints procedures
- Crisis/contingency systems

Some more specialised systems, not used by every organisation, will have direct effect where they exist. These include:

- Shipping/import/export
- Membership
- Booking

Each of these systems is complementary to a system in the customer's organisation. Sales systems are matched by purchasing systems; supply systems by receiving systems; supplier accounting systems by customer accounting systems and so on.

The match between pairs of systems is of great importance in giving customer service. It is not enough that our systems work well; they must fit well with those of our customers. The interface at which data are exchanged, either in writing, by personal contact or by computer, must work smoothly. But more than that, when the data have been exchanged, they must be appropriate for and in suitable form for our customer's systems. In a phrase, our systems must be 'customer friendly'.

Other systems will not have a direct interface with the customer's systems, but will nevertheless have a major impact on the service he receives. These include:

- Sales forecasting
- Production planning and control
- Inventory control

The effect of these systems on the satisfaction of orders, and hence on the level of customer service, may be paramount. However, their workings are usually hidden. It is outside the scope of this book to do more than emphasise their importance.

There are other, less common systems which will, where they exist, have an effect on customer service. These include:

- Engineering/design
- Research and development
- Road fleet management

As computerisation and information technology moves forward, more organisations of all sizes are integrating several systems into one, as for example, by linking ordering, stock control and accounting systems. This approach usually offers both advantages and snags. The advantages are mainly for the supplier, but the automatic transfer of information without human intervention may have something to offer the customer, in the form of fewer mistakes and perhaps greater speed of response. The snags are the likelihood that if mistakes do occur they may be bigger and much harder to rectify, and that the bigger the system the less flexible it will be to special or changing requirements.

Sales/ordering systems

These include order entry, invoicing, sales ledger, and salesmen's visit systems.

This is an area in which internal conflict is endemic: the conflict between the sales force keen for the order and the rest of the organisation tasked with delivering the order. Selling matters to every organisation, but only if the goods are delivered as ordered. If they are not, the very act of selling becomes, in the long term, counter-productive.

Promises about expected delivery come into this area. Organisations which leave this to the whims of over-optimistic sales people can only store up trouble for themselves. Internal instructions and disciplines need to be effective. Consumer protection organisations are moving into this area.

Order quantities, price breaks and packaging methods can be planned with the customer in mind. Customer needs will vary, but the majority must get what they need. Where additional costs must be incurred by the supplier to provide this convenience, it may be that many customers, given the choice, would be prepared to pay.

When repeat ordering by a regular customer is involved, salesmen are less likely to play a role, and the customer may be expected to deal direct with an order-taking department. Ease and accuracy of ordering will always be important, but may be harder to achieve. The documentation required may be troublesome for the customer, or may not cover every eventuality. Whether and in what circumstances telephone orders are accepted may need to be defined.

Computer (and indeed manual) systems can be planned to match those of customers. With large customers, there should, these days, be little difficulty; computer to computer ordering has been with us technically for some time, and offers big advantages for regular trading partners. Even many smaller customers can be helped by careful design of the parts of a system (such as ordering and invoicing procedures) that must form an interface.

The customer can be offered even more positive help by well designed systems that have, for example, built-in checks against unusual or over-size orders.

The question of how to handle panic or priority orders may need to be faced. To be able to meet these is clearly a great service to the customer receiving the order, but may easily harm the service to others. The biggest problem is that if the procedure is too easy to invoke it will be used more and more frequently and eventually come to replace the standard procedure. A simple expedient may be to offer such a service at a premium rate.

Order status information

Customers of all kinds may, for their own valid reasons, need to know where their order is at any time. If the delivery promise or the expected time has not been met, they are fully entitled to be told what has happened and when their goods or service will be provided. In these circumstances, there is every reason to suggest that the supplier has an obligation to initiate communication rather than merely to react.

This is an area of endless failure, and one in which suppliers with systems that can supply accurate order-status information whenever it is needed, proactively in case of delay, must have a huge marketing advantage.

Supply/logistics systems

These include all aspects of physical distribution, or logistics, as it is now frequently called; those systems that must actually move the goods from supplier to customer; warehousing, transport, and the associated flows of information.

This area has developed greatly in importance in recent years, and many suppliers regard it as the key to better customer service. From relatively simple transport management has grown an area of increasing sophistication and complexity, with entirely new standards of performance. The growth of computer-based information technology has had a big influence in several aspects; it has enabled stockholdings to be reduced and the control of transport fleets to be improved. Many organisations have substantially cut the number of their warehouses while improving delivery to customers.

There has been a massive growth of specialised organisations offering complete distribution services, often on a contracted basis. Road vehicles may be painted in clients' liveries. In some cases, services of great speed and accuracy (including accepted penalties in case of failure) may be offered at premium rates.

For the customer, good logistics are measured by time, accuracy and condition of the goods (or service).

Time matters to the customer in two ways, absolute and relative.

Absolute time matters in that the system must operate without what customers perceive to be unreasonable delay. What is perceived as unreasonable will vary depending on the nature of the operation and how rapidly competitive and similar operations are completed.

The wise provider needs to know as accurately as possible what are his customers' expectations with regard to speed of delivery. Most of us accept a wait when we have ordered a special meal; some are prepared to wait a bit longer than others, but there is a minimum delay which (in given circumstances) everyone would accept, and a maximum beyond which we would all walk out. The same is true in all other customer situations. The trap is to miss changes in expectations. People who would accept delivery in a month last year may have come to expect it within days this year, especially if a new supplier can achieve this.

The length of time taken by the operation itself is not the only variable; the arrival of customers in batches or peaks may give rise to queueing. This is an unavoidable risk in any customer service situation, and is generally accepted by normally patient customers in that spirit. However, the more frequent and the longer the queues, the fewer customers will accept them as inevitable, and the more will seek alternative suppliers.

Providing a service on demand may well present insuperable problems. The restaurant that could serve every customer as soon as he arrived would be uneconomically large, too generously equipped and grossly overstaffed. The theatre that could always offer the seat we wanted would be full of empty seats most of the time.

Minimising queueing *may* require additional resources, but this automatic reaction is often unjustified. The situation is always worth careful study, and there may be approaches which can offer highly cost-effective relief in return for a little clear and creative thinking.

There may be bottlenecks—points in the system where the flow of work is slower than elsewhere—which can be eliminated at little or no additional cost. The provision of fast checkouts in supermarkets and joint queues for all tills in banks are excellent examples of this.

In some situations, relief can be found by educating the customer to avoid the periods of peak demand.

In others, a price incentive or other bonus for the customer may help to spread the load more evenly.

Operational Research offers the technique known as 'queueing theory', which provides answers on a statistical basis to questions of queueing. The mathematics is not complex, and if queueing remains a problem it will be worth using the technique to establish what effect various options would have on the service offered, and compare this with any additional capital or running costs.

Relative time. Relative time matters as much to customers as absolute time. A rapid system of letter handling or milk delivery that reaches the customer in the middle of the day is of less value than a slower system that achieves delivery before breakfast.

Opening and closing hours fall into this category. The post office that insists on its lunch break may add hours or days to the effective speed of its systems for those customers that can only get there in *their* lunch break. Museums and art galleries that close at weekends might just as well not be there for much of the population; fast buses that start when no one wants to travel are effectively slower than slow buses at the best time.

The optimum stock level. Holding stocks to meet any demand would be (a) incredibly costly, and in any case (b) virtually impossible. Stockholding costs money in several ways; capital is locked up useless in the goods that are waiting and must be paid for at current rates of interest; the goods must be stored in suitable conditions, protected and insured; movement into and out of store costs money, and there is the danger that obsolescence can overtake the stored goods, lowering the value or even making them unsaleable.

Wrong stock levels have probably caused more bankruptcy than any other single error. If they are too low, customers will go to other suppliers who can meet their needs. If they are too high, the problems listed in the last paragraph can easily prove fatal. It is beyond the scope of this book to indicate detailed approaches, which in any case will be very specific to each kind of business. But this is one of the critical areas not only of customer service but of all business, and deserves the most careful and continuing management attention.

Just in time. From the provider of raw material to the ultimate user of a product there is a chain. This is known either as the 'supply chain' or the 'demand chain', depending on which motivating forces are being considered. An inefficient chain will work slowly and jerkily, with bottlenecks and pools of unwanted products in storage. The ideal chain will work at the same pace throughout its length.

The philosophy of 'just in time' (or 'kanban', the Japanese term) is of great importance in some operations. With this approach, the aim is to supply goods at the point of use as nearly as possible just before they are needed. The same aim may be set at each stage back through the demand chain.

This calls for totally new standards of accuracy, and a new breed of specialised organisations is springing up to meet them. Some carriers now accept penalties based not on the number of hours but the number of minutes by which they fail to deliver at a predetermined time.

Just-in-time requires the most detailed knowledge of the customer's needs and circumstances, iron discipline, good contingency planning and a continuous stream of accurate information. It is an approach which, while still comparatively rare in its pure form, is having an ever-increasing influence on delivery expectations.

Accounting systems

These include credit control, invoicing, cashier and debt collection systems.

The principal need from the customer's angle is accuracy. No amount of mechanisation removes the need for human intervention. Indeed, mistakes, once made, may be much harder to rectify. Suppliers who send inaccurate invoices, let alone reminders and final notices, will lose whatever goodwill the other elements of the transaction have generated. Good systems must ensure that the computer does not take over.

Manual credit card systems are rather customer unfriendly, with their clumsy and time-consuming documentation. On the other hand, on-line cash dispensing and accounting systems present a classic case of a product-driven system. Designed to meet the needs of the supplier (bank, building society or trader) they are then sold to the customer. The need for compatibility and standardisation inevitably lessens further the chances that the customer's preferences can affect the design of the system.

In the retail sector, the bar-coding of goods offers the possibility of accounting automation, and the information gathered at the point of sale can be used for sales statistics and stock control.

In both these cases, the customer may benefit indirectly from a more effective supply chain (of money or products), but any direct benefit at the point of use is a matter of chance.

After-sales service systems

These include systems for spares and consumables, stock control and control of service engineers' visits.

The common problems of delayed visits by service engineers and lack of necessary spares are a key area for customer service improvement. Standards vary widely; some organisations go to immense lengths, such as despatching service personnel to any part of the world on demand; others do nothing.

In the US, some organisations are prepared to advertise and accept penalties if they fail to achieve specified speeds of response; this approach might offer a marketing edge to those willing to adopt it in the UK.

Some parts can, with advantage, be supplied and packaged to meet the way in which the customer will use them; 'kits' of related parts may be made up to meet most needs. On the other hand, individual parts must be readily available for customers whose requirement is unusual.

The holding of spares for obsolete products will remain a problem, but a hawkish policy of clearing out may lose much customer goodwill. Apart from the difficulties with current equipment, the feeling will be generated that pressure for new purchasing is being unfairly applied. Sometimes independent agencies may see the opportunity to fill this gap, if given full co-operation by manufacturers.

Complaints procedures

Complaints handling is a mix of systems and interpersonal skills.

The systems must allow proper investigation and recording of complaints without excessive bureaucracy. They must give staff clear rules for settlement, placing explicit authority in the hands of those who may be involved. They must respond very quickly, as there is much research indicating that speed of response may be even more important to the customer than acceptance or rejection.

These procedures are discussed more fully in Chapter 9.

Crisis systems

Irish coffee, so the story goes, was given to a waiting world by a caring and creative airline one foul winter night at Shannon Airport, when a plane-load of passengers was unable to take off on their transatlantic flight. While the facts are not on record, it seems likely that the passengers involved in this historic event have for ever blessed rather than cursed the delay they suffered.

The weary businessman arriving after a hard day at his hotel learns from the receptionist that the booking has been mishandled, and there is no room for him. So far, so bad, but what really matters is what happens next. At the least failing in courtesy and concern, a solicitor's letter will soon be on its way, and a bitter ex-customer will be spreading the word to everyone he meets.

But sit that same customer immediately on a sofa with a large complimentary drink in his hand, send the duty manager to apologise personally to him while a receptionist completes arrangements with another hotel, and send him at length down the road to an establishment with at least one extra star in its rating, and the customer will feel greater satisfaction than if nothing had gone wrong.

Systems of every kind are liable to go wrong. If they do not fail for internal reasons, nothing can eliminate the risk of outside difficulties: bad weather, failed crops, strikes, earthquakes or other 'acts of God'. The bad organisation throws in its hand at this point; the good organisation sees such events as heaven-sent opportunities to impress customers with their caring and efficient service.

To achieve these effects, contingency plans must exist, and systems must have been set up to cope with the unexpected. This is not really too difficult to arrange.

If in fact the truly unexpected occurs (as opposed to the merely less common occurrences, such as snow in winter) then everything will depend on the attitude and ingenuity of the staff who must help the customer.

The problems of changing systems

Changing or getting rid of ineffective systems is a difficult task. There are several reasons for this:

- Large systems represent an investment of much time and capital. Modern electronic systems, depending on expensive hardware and even more expensive software are for this reason even harder to change than older systems.
- Change takes time from day-to-day work which can be ill spared.
- Development and implementation of improved systems, whether electronic or manual, demands specialist skills of a high order.
- Use of well-known systems is far easier for those working with them than living with change, and gives a sense of security.
- Better systems may need fewer staff, thus posing problems of redundancy, relocation or retraining.

Large systems can be so resistant to change that they may destroy the organisation that created them.

These problems have sometimes led to rather grotesque and desperate strategies. Occasionally, it has seemed to be easier to cut off those parts of an organisation with bad systems than to improve their systems; to close branches or branch lines, for example. Another stratagem has been to relocate an operation, thus losing a high proportion of the staff and giving the chance to start with a slate clean of both systems and staff. Commonest of all is the introduction of new technology, which provides an opening for systems which may, in some cases, have been introduced to greater advantage without the technology.

The well-managed organisation will avoid all these mistakes, and set about changing systems rationally. In every case, the need is to review the system to establish what effect it has on customer service. For those that have an effect, the questions to be answered are:

- Is the system needed at all?
- Does it work well internally?
- Is it customer-friendly?
- Can it be simplified?
- Can it be combined or integrated?
- Can it be mechanised?

Changes may not only affect customer service performance; if we are lucky, they may improve internal efficiency or reduce cost. If we are not, they may have the reverse effect, when we shall have to judge whether or not they are worth making.

Who can best help?

Changing systems of any size or complexity is a specialist job. Several sources are available:

- External consultants
- Internal specialists
- Detached executives
- Departmental staff
- Suggestion schemes
- Trainees
- Customers
- Try it yourself

External consultants
The steps in the choice and use of an external consultant are described in Chapter 13; here it is perhaps only necessary to emphasise that their greatest advantage is their detachment from internal pressures and politics, and the opportunity this gives them to make unpopular recommendations.

Internal specialists
Internal consultants may well be part of the situation they are studying; they may have partial, incorrect or outdated knowledge of the systems in question, thus making a fresh, unbiased look far harder to achieve; and they will certainly find it harder to tell those involved, especially at a senior level, that they are wrong.

Detached executives
The use of a senior executive, specially detached from other duties,

has much to recommend it provided the right person can be found.

Such a person will have the authority necessary to give him access to all levels and departments; will have a good perspective of the whole operation; and will have the ear of those who can ensure that his recommendations have the best chance of success.

Departmental staff

Departmental staff can be used provided management are mature and secure enough not to feel threatened by criticism or proposed change, and other departments also do not see changes as a challenge or a threat.

Suggestion schemes

Suggestion schemes have produced startling benefits for some organisations. But because they operate outside the normal process of management, they can be held at arm's length by staff and treated with suspicion by managers.

Trainees

Like the use of detached senior executives, this is heavily dependent on the choice of individuals. The most frequent choice is a young high-flier which almost always benefits the individual more than the organisation. At worst, it can be counter-productive, by generating resentment and resistance to the changes proposed, and widening the gap perceived between trainees and others.

Customers

Customers have to work with our systems, and may, in many cases, be the best people to help us make them customer-friendly.

Some organisations are prepared to offer a suggestion scheme to their customers. This may be of real value to retailers and other organisations who have many thousands of customers with whom individual communication would be difficult; organisations with smaller numbers should have a relationship with their customers that makes suggestions on better service welcome at all times.

One of the more remarkable examples of system-planning from the customer's angle was devised by the Nationwide Building Society, which took double full-page advertisements in the national press. One of the pages explained the area of operation in which the Society wished to develop new systems; the facing page was blank, and readers were invited to use it to describe their criteria for that area, and the sort of system they would like to see.

Systems (such as ordering and invoicing systems) which have a direct interface with customer systems must always be a legitimate area for discussion. In doing so, we are not asking the customer to tell us how to conduct our business, but looking for methods which will be of mutual benefit and at the same time give us the marketing advantage of customer-friendliness.

In the case of a public service, many internal systems will be fully visible to the customer. Perhaps the clearest example is a passenger transport system. Railway officers are wont to complain that their customers invariably feel they can run the railway better than they do. Setting aside any possible grain of truth in such an assertion, the principal reason for this is that railway customers have access to the 'factory' every time they travel. This is an uncomfortable situation, but it does have the advantage that the advice of customers will at least be better informed.

Try it yourself
In the last analysis, the best move in many situations may be to see our systems literally from the customer's point of view. How many suppliers ever fill in their own order forms, or use their other systems as a customer? This should not be too difficult; we are all someone's customer, and if we cannot easily buy from our own company it is likely that our family, friends or close and trusted associates may do so to test the system.

Simple and effective changes may often best be seen in this way. Forms may be redesigned for customer convenience. Manuals and instruction books can be compiled to answer the customer's questions, in the order he is likely to ask them, not as an extra selling aid listing the manufacturer's features. Supermarket shelves can be arranged to stock products in an order which is convenient and meaningful to the shopper rather than to the filler.

Customer training

Where complex or difficult systems are unavoidable, the customer may need help by training, through leaflets or manuals, open days at which they can visit and talk to supplier staff, seminars or even training courses. Buyers or new customers may well benefit from and welcome the opportunity to meet those they will work with of the supplier's staff and see how and where they work. Not only will the formal systems run more smoothly, but helpful and informal relationships can be formed that will oil the wheels.

Thought-starters

1. What systems operated by other organisations have struck you as particularly customer-unfriendly? How would you improve them?
2. What are the principal systems you are involved with? Which of these affect customer service, and is the effect direct or indirect?
3. Have these systems been reviewed for customer-friendliness? If so, what was the result; if not, what would you expect to be the likely results of such a review?

Action points

1. Establish priority order system at premium rate (page 156).
2. Upgrade logistics systems or use specialist contractors (pages 156-9).
3. Examine systems for bottlenecks and take action to eliminate them (page 158).
4. Check opening and closing hours and delivery times for customer convenience (page 158).
5. Offer guaranteed servicing call-out time (page 160).
6. Set up contingency plans for crisis service (pages 161-2).

13
THE CUSTOMER SERVICE SURVEY

TO ACHIEVE LASTING and methodical improvement in our customer service, we must do everything practicable to learn about the present situation; above all, about what our customers want. The more time we can devote to this phase, and the more systematic we can be, the stronger our foundation will be for subsequent action.

It may be felt that to carry out a major survey of this kind is only appropriate for larger organisations. This is emphatically not the case. A one-person organisation can gain tremendous benefit from such an exercise. But for all sizes of organisation, there is the option of devoting resources to a full survey, or settling for something less. Knowledge of the service our customers want is so important that this is an area in which a little knowledge is not necessarily dangerous; it is a good deal better than none at all.

This chapter discusses first the knowledge we need to have and some of the difficulties in obtaining and interpreting it. It then suggests the options of a mini survey, or a full survey carried out either by the market research department, a specially assembled in-house team, or by external consultants.

The knowledge we must have

There are three areas about which we must gain accurate knowledge:

- What service do we currently give our customers?
- What service do customers (existing and potential) want?
- What service do our competitors give?

Each of these is now considered in more detail.

What service do we currently give our customers?
This should be the easiest area to explore, although there are some important barriers to accurate knowledge which make commonly held views untrustworthy as a basis for action:

- Weak anecdotal evidence, often based on single incidents, will be given far too much weight.
- The problems of those customers who complain, which may be atypical, are not counterbalanced by the views of those who do not.
- Many badly served customers will not complain. If they have a choice, they will go elsewhere, some sooner, some later. If the organisation is in a monopoly position, they will become disaffected and await the chance of registering their feelings, sometimes after many years and in very damaging ways.
- The opinions of small numbers of strongly articulate customers, especially if of high status, personally known to top management, or expressed through the public media, will be given too much weight.
- Preconceptions within the organisation about its customer service standing may be badly out of date or mistaken in other ways.

What is needed are objective measures of each specific area of customer service. Data on some or all of these may already exist, although we shall be lucky if it is easily accessible, or in the form we want.

What service do our customers, existing and potential, want?
This second area is harder to explore, as it involves some kind of systematic fact-gathering outside our organisation. Two points need to be borne in mind:

1. Customer service is a matter of perception. Customer service is, in the last analysis, a matter of perception.

The primary goods or services provided by the organisation can be measured objectively. They can be weighed, measured, their operation checked, their material analysed. Secondary, or customer service may certainly be measured, but its value to the customer is subjective.

Delivery, for example, may be said to be 'slow'. Delivery, then, is obviously felt to be slower than it should be in the particular circumstances, but slower against what benchmark? Is it slower than the delivery achieved by competitors, the speed of our previous deliveries, a promise made by the organisation, or some general feeling, possibly based on quite different products or situations?

It is the *feeling* that counts. As with normal social situations, we build up a subjective pattern of limits of tolerance, which varies between individuals within wide limits. Some of us are impatient if a friend is even a minute late; some only start to feel bad if they are more than half an hour behind time. If we are both due to catch the same plane, or if we are waiting in the rain, lateness feels different from a wait in a comfortable bar or in front of our own fire.

Again, 'lack of information' about our product may be a complaint. But how much information do we reasonably need to provide? A performance specification, prices and delivery, a picture, a full set of drawings, instructions for use, maintenance and servicing details, materials specification, comparisons with competitive products, history of our organisation, qualifications of our personnel, comments of other users... It is difficult to draw a line that will always satisfy everyone. The only ultimate guide can be the perceptions our customers and prospective customers hold about the amount of information they need.

Nowhere is the subjective nature of customer service clearer than in the field of behaviour. Many of the bitterest arguments and strongest feelings arise from allegations of 'rudeness'. But as all who have ever been involved, on either side of the problem, know, such an allegation is nearly impossible to prove. If there are witnesses, it may be possible to prove what words were used, but the tone of voice, the body language and the context will be much harder to pin down, and the attitudes and expectations of the parties involved could only be guessed at by a psychiatrist.

Throughout each aspect of customer service, the same is true; we are dealing with facts, certainly, but measuring them against feelings, expectations and perceptions. What seems a good level of service to us, the provider, may be perceived as poor and inadequate by the customer or potential customer. Equally, it may be seen as excessive; we may be over-providing.

Customer perceptions and expectations also vary over time, and according to what the competition can offer. A one-week delivery may have been perceived as good enough, until our latest competitor was able to achieve reliable two-day delivery.

2. *Customers vary.* The relative importance to the customer of the elements of customer service, and the standards achieved in each, may vary within wide limits. Customer A may run a business in which reliability of delivery to within the hour is vital; customer B may need an unusual range of financial options; customer C may require the highest standards of after-sales support.

It may be possible to classify our customers by type; to consider the service we give by market segment, geographical area, size of account, or some other variable. Our research may show that there are differences which we can exploit by offering levels of service which match the needs of particular sectors, possibly withdrawing from others or increasing our charges to an economical level.

In some cases, it is possible that the standards required are higher than we can economically offer. In others, we may be wasting resources in doing more than is needed; our service may be better than some customers or sectors want; we may be pouring water into the sand.

Export markets may offer a clear case for segmentation. It is easy to assume that customers in each country share the same customer service priorities, but this may prove to be quite incorrect.

What service do our competitors give?

Facts about the service provided by the competition may be even harder to obtain, but here also the effort is likely to be of great value. They will tell us our relative position in the league of customer service; where we must improve and where we may be wasting resources.

If a full survey is not conducted, it may be necessary to obtain as much information as possible from published documents, the knowledge of our own staff (especially the sales force) and possibly informal contacts with long-standing customers.

The areas to be researched are the same as for our own service.

Conducting a mini survey

As suggested at the beginning of the chapter, while there can be no doubt of the value of full information, there may be strong pressures of time and cost which make a full survey impracticable. If this is felt to be the case, the option of conducting a mini survey may be attractive. This can, in any case, be undertaken when the area of customer service is being systematically explored for the first time, in order to build up experience.

If a mini survey is chosen, then the procedure should follow steps 6 to 10 of the in-house survey described below, except that the final step should include the presentation of conclusions on which further action can be based.

Planning a full customer service survey

If we can call on the services of a marketing department equipped to undertake market research, we should have few problems; the skills for undertaking the customer service survey will be found there. If not, outside consultants may be used; this is discussed below. If neither of these is suitable, it may be possible to undertake the work from a specially assembled in-house team. In a small organisation, one person may be able to carry out the survey, given a readiness to learn and use the necessary skills.

The survey can be combined with wider market research, including the primary products or services offered by the organisation. This combination is logical, but may have practical problems. It may result either in too large and clumsy an exercise being undertaken, unacceptable delays while all departments involved are brought together, or the customer service angle becoming submerged by other aspects.

Apart from providing the good, disinterested evidence required, such a survey may offer bonuses of involving customers, thus giving it a marketing dimension, and of developing the skills of staff by involving them and giving them a learning experience.

The survey may present resource problems, including the cost, sparing staff from their existing duties, and finding the necessary skills. These will need to be taken into consideration in deciding which method to adopt, and how extensive the exercise can be.

In-house survey

If it is decided to use a specially assembled in-house team to complete the survey, a typical plan would include the following steps:

1. Obtain and demonstrate the commitment of top management to the exercise.
2. Define the objectives of the exercise accurately and in writing.

3. Choose a leader (and members, if the size of the exercise justifies it) of the survey team with great care. In the absence of staff who are skilled in survey work, someone must be chosen who is able and willing to find and use advice and information about this work and to be trained if necessary in the appropriate skills. They must also be highly articulate, acceptable to the widest range of people, methodical and intelligent. Strong departmental loyalty or long experience in particular areas of the organisation are definite drawbacks.

4. Consult all concerned face to face, individually or in groups, depending on numbers and any laid-down procedures for staff consultation. Explain the objectives, obtain comment and feedback on these and incorporate or adapt as appropriate. Talk about and agree the method to be followed, but do not allow discussion at this stage of the actual subject matter of the survey.

5. Arrange clearly the level and method of reporting of the conclusions to avoid as far as possible departmental limitations and internal political pressures.

The following five steps should be followed in a mini survey

6. Make a provisional analysis of the organisation's customers, deciding whether they may fall into categories with differing service expectations. In doing this, consider factors such as the goods or services bought, amount spent over time, size of individual transactions, frequency of transactions, length of business connection with the organisation, experience of competitors, geographical location, nationality, sex, age, and ethnic or socio-economic groups.

7. Design a questionnaire to be used in customer interviewing (during the pilot phase of the survey). At this stage, a simple, largely open-ended approach is desirable. This will help the interviewees to focus on the subject of the survey, enlist their active support, help them to think and talk freely, and obtain the maximum insight into their own perceptions of and expectations from customer service. The areas to be explored will include:

● The primary products or services for which the individual is a customer

- The length of time during which he has bought from the organisation
- The approximate level of value of his purchases in a typical period of time
- What elements the customer perceives as part of the service which the organisation does or should offer to him. Some judicious prompting is allowable at this stage, but only to get thinking channelled and flowing in the right direction.
  - Do we supply sufficient information?
  - Is our ordering procedure and other paperwork convenient?
  - Do our terms of finance meet his needs?
  - Are order quantities and delivery frequencies suitable?
  - What speed of order fulfilment do we achieve, and is this appropriate?
  - How often and by how much do we fail on delivery promises?
  - How accurate are our orders, in number and items? Are they delivered free from damage?
  - What is the standard of our customer contact face to face, by letter and by telephone?
  - Is our complaints handling efficient, fair and speedy?
  - What standards of after-sales service do we achieve? What is the response time to calls for service and repair? What level of part availability do we achieve, are consumables readily available? Do we readily offer advice and support?
  - What order of importance does the customer attach to each of the elements he has identified?
  - Aspects of customer service provided by competitors but not by this organisation, or provided differently, and the effect of these differences.

8. Choose a small sample of customers from each category. The size of the sample will depend at this stage on the total number in the category; the aim should be a minimum of 20 from each. The choice of customers within the category should be made by a method which avoids bias; depending on circumstances, a table of random numbers can be applied to a list.

   Depending on the nature of the organisation and its

business, customers will need to be approached personally, by letter, or by telephone. If personal interviews are used, interviewers will need careful briefing in techniques to avoid bias in choosing their sample or interpreting the answers.

9. Obtain data from the sample, recording the results methodically.

10. Analyse the records with three objectives:

- To recheck and amend the provisional categorisation of customers.
- To produce a workable listing of the dimensions of customer service perceived by the customers of the organisation, including *both* those that are currently provided *and* those that are felt to be needed.
- To make an initial identification of the differences in customer service between this organisation and its competitors.

This would normally conclude the work necessary for a mini survey.

11. Devise a second questionnaire to be used during the main phase of the survey. This should cover the same ground as the pilot survey, but the exploration of the perception of the elements of customer service, their relative importance, and the differences with competitors should be made by the use (with ticking or numbering) of carefully designed lists or forced-choice questions.

The approach at this stage is no longer aimed at open-ended discussion, but at the acquisition of tight and measurable data for subsequent analysis. The possibility of computer analysis should be borne in mind; if the number of completed surveys is likely to exceed a few hundred this is virtually essential.

12. Arrange completion of a small number of questionnaires under working conditions, either by the interviewers, if these are to be used, or by sample customers, if the questionnaires are for postal or self-completion. Make any necessary adjustments to debug and ensure smooth and efficient working.

13. Using the refined categorisation of customers, plan the samples for the full survey. Statistical advice may be needed in complex cases. Ensure that balanced coverage

of non-customers is provided by some appropriate technique, possibly based on mailing lists or directories.

14. Conduct the survey. The first choice must always be to use face-to-face interviews. If this is too time-consuming or expensive, self-completion, possibly with postal distribution and/or collection, may be chosen. However, this has the drawbacks of substantially reducing the response rate (which may easily fall below 10 per cent), possibly introducing bias into the sample, and reducing accuracy of completion.

15. Analyse the results. Appropriate statistical techniques will be necessary to interpret the results. Expert advice should be sought, unless the team has the knowledge.

16. Using the data from the survey and any other sources, answer the questions; who are our customers?; what customer service do they require?; what customer service do we give them?; what service do our competitors give?; what is the cost of our customer services?

17. Present the results in a meaningful and easily assimilated form upon which action can be based. It is usually best to present not only in written report form, but also orally.

Consultant survey

Unless the resources of a marketing department are available, a full survey is a major project, and the possibility of engaging external specialists will need to be considered.

Even where a marketing department exists, there may be advantages in using outside help. These may include the additional manpower and special expertise provided, and the freedom to report findings which may be critical of policy, departments or of individuals at any level.

The disadvantages of using external consultants include the difficulty of choosing specialists with appropriate expertise and the substantial costs that may be involved.

The steps in the mounting of a consultant customer service survey will usually include:

1. Obtain and demonstrate the commitment of top management to the exercise.

2. Define the objectives of the exercise accurately and in

writing. Consider in particular whether the use of external advice offers the opportunity to survey not only your organisation's effectiveness, but also to make informed comparisons with competitors.

3. Obtain from a reliable source the names of consultants specialising in this kind of work. Professional and trade bodies, professional institutes and reference libraries can provide guidance of this sort. Some will also give recommendations, but usually only to organisations or individuals who are members. Personal recommendations from reliable contacts are, as always, of great value at this preliminary stage, although the prudent manager will always aim to form his own judgement as soon as possible.

4. Contact a number to arrange preliminary discussions. It is often possible to clear much ground in a first telephone conversation, although any worthwhile consultant will be entirely happy to visit and discuss an assignment which seems to be within their area of expertise without cost or obligation. It is essential to exchange as much information as possible at this stage. A summary should be given of the organisation and its business (if not already well known to the consultants), the role of the person giving the briefing, the objectives of the assignment as currently seen, the format of the desired conclusions, and any constraints of time, money or internal politics. If more than one firm of consultants is being approached (and it is best this should be so), this should, in fairness be made clear to each.

In return, the consultant should be expected to give full information about his own firm; its size (but remember that largeness is not by any means an advantage; small, specialised firms or even individuals may do better than large, all-can-do organisations—most depends on the consultant himself), ownership and the work it has undertaken (references to other clients should be willingly offered), who will undertake the various stages of the assignment and their personal experience and background, and the outline stages through which the assignment will be tackled. It is best practice if the consultant taking the first briefing is the one who will personally lead the assignment—this should be checked at first meeting. Any reliable

consultant will give immediate feedback as to whether the
assignment is one they are able and willing to undertake.

5. Receive and study proposals from the consultants. These
   may be presented verbally, which is best, as it gives
   opportunity for questioning and further personal assessment of the consultant, and the all-important 'body
   chemistry' between him and you. The proposals should
   indicate a clear understanding of the nature of the
   organisation and the purposes and constraints of the
   assignment, should lay out the stages to be followed and
   the time-scale for the completion of each, should specify
   the individual consultants who will do the work, and give a
   clear and unambiguous indication of cost and the nature of
   the contractual obligation throughout the stages.

   Proposals should always also be presented in writing for
   further study. The written proposals should be clear and
   well-presented, but judgement must be made on the
   content rather than the glossiness of the package.

6. Follow up the references to previous clients offered,
   bearing in mind the similarity (or differences) in the
   organisations and the work done for them. Face-to-face or
   telephone discussion is best, and what is not said is often
   as important as what is said. Obviously a reference to
   someone personally known is particularly valuable. A good
   referee will be ready and prepared to answer methodical
   and probing questions on any areas of doubt; if they are
   not, ask the consultant for other referees.

7. Choose the consultant to be engaged, if necessary after
   further questioning and discussions with those who are
   likely choices. Good consultants will not be tight or
   defensive in their pre-assignment contacts, as full understanding with a client is essential to success in an
   assignment. At every stage, be sensitive to the personal
   relationship developing between the consultant and you
   and the others with whom he would have to work; these are
   at least as important as the purely technical skills and
   knowledge displayed. Cost levels may prove to vary
   widely; it is important, as with other goods and services,
   not to shop by price, and to ensure that like is being
   compared with like. If none of the consultants appears able
   or willing to do what is needed, or if the level of costs

proves to be too high, tell them so. Do not, however, give in to a temptation to pick a consultant's brains and then ditch him; word will get around, and good help will prove difficult to get on a future occasion.

8. Tie up the contract for the assignment in a good, water-tight contract fair to both parties and covering every foreseeable problem.

9. Consult all concerned within the organisation face to face, individually or in groups depending on numbers and any laid-down procedures for staff consultation. Introduce the consultants. Explain the objectives, obtain comment and feedback on these and incorporate or adapt as appropriate. Talk about and agree the method to be followed, but do not allow discussion at this stage of the actual subject matter of the survey.

10. Arrange clearly the level and method of progressing the assignment and reporting conclusions to avoid as far as possible departmental limitations and internal political pressures. Ensure that the consultants know for whom they are working, and to whom they can go for advice and contacts.

11. Ensure that the conclusions are well presented to all who need to know, working with the consultants to get maximum impact from their work.

Thought-starters

1. Do you know the levels of customer service your organisation is currently achieving; what levels your customers want, and how they perceive what they are getting; and what levels your competitors achieve? Is your knowledge up to date?

2. Is it possible to classify your customers into different segments according to their customer service needs? If so, what might these be? Does your organisation already do this, and if not, might it be an advantage?

3. Has your organisation the skills and resources to carry out a customer service survey? Are you convinced it could be cost-effective to do so?

Action point

Conduct a customer service full or mini survey.

14
THE IMPROVEMENT PLAN

IF WE ARE committed to upgrading our organisation's customer service to the highest level, this will, like other major changes, require the most thorough planning. Piecemeal improvements may help, but are unlikely to go far in changing the long-term philosophy and drive of the organisation, and may rapidly be swamped by other pressures.

In particular, it is very unlikely that an isolated programme of front-line staff training will by itself achieve worthwhile and lasting results. Such a programme must be supported by much deeper changes. These changes may, indeed, have to cross the border from service to the primary product itself; in the last analysis good service cannot be supported indefinitely on the basis of a bad product (or primary service).

As was suggested in Chapter 11, the best starting point for thorough-going change is likely to be a clear declaration of policy, developed in consultation with everyone who will have to carry it out, endorsed at top level, and published for all to see.

Also in Chapter 11, it was suggested that functional control of all aspects of customer service should be vested in a director or senior executive with direct access to the top of the organisation. The way that control should be exercised, whether he should be supported by a department, and if so the duties of that department will depend on the size and nature of the organisation.

In Chapter 13, the value of a customer service survey was emphasised, whether a full survey or the less demanding but useful mini survey. The data produced by this will provide the springboard for the remaining steps necessary to formulate a viable and comprehensive improvement plan, and put it into action.

Any thorough-going survey is likely to have thrown up a number of quite specific issues of varying seriousness. Some may be so clear-cut that they call for action as soon as they are brought to light. We may have learnt, for example, that a particular member of our staff is not dealing with documentation correctly, that the packaging of one of our products renders it difficult to store and handle, or that our new fare structure is completely misunderstood by the public. We do not need to wait for a plan to take action on these, even though the causes of the problems may be part of the overall picture we will examine.

The five steps

There are five further steps through to completion of our improvement plan:

1. Defining problem areas
2. Choosing solutions
3. Setting the improvement plan in action
4. Changing attitudes and behaviour by training
5. Monitoring results

Defining problem areas

If we have been able to collect data on the basis of different market segments, as suggested in Chapter 13, a natural starting point will be to set out our data by service element and market segment, constructing a matrix such as this, which might be produced by a manufacturer.

| Dimension of service | Market sector | | | |
	Large Accounts	Small Accounts (South)	Small Accounts (North)	Export Accounts
Order processing and documentation	3	3	3	1
Speed of delivery	3	3	1	3
Freedom from damage	3	3	3	3
Reliability of delivery	3	2*	0*	2
Complaints handling	2*	2*	0*	1
After sales service	1	1	0*	3
Staff helpfulness	1	1	1	3

3=very satisfactory   2=fairly satisfactory   1=not very satisfactory
0=unsatisfactory   *=known to be below competition

Several problem areas are suggested:

1. Large accounts and small accounts (South) are effectively not separate segments.
2. Small accounts (North) is clearly a separate segment, and suffers serious problems.
3. Export accounts have several problems.
4. After-sales service is a major problem area.
5. Export staff are very helpful; all others apparently need attention of some sort.
6. Large accounts may be being over-serviced.
7. Packaging might be too lavish.

A local bus service might produce a matrix:

	Market sector		
Dimension of service	School service	Party hire	Route 1
Punctuality	2	2*	2
Cleanliness	0	3	2
Staff helpfulness	0	1*	2
Customer information	3	3	1

3=very satisfactory   2=fairly satisfactory   1=not very satisfactory
0=unsatisfactory   *=known to be below competition

The problems suggested might be:

1. All three sectors are very different in service needs and levels.
2. Party hire business is under serious threat from competition.
3. All three sectors present problems.
4. The school service may be under threat when contracts are due for renewal.
5. Staff helpfulness appears to need attention.

Matrices of this type highlight problem areas, but we shall need to examine the survey data and any other sources of information to establish the nature and possible causes of the problems.

Choosing solutions
Cause finding. Solutions will never work if applied to symptoms or to assumed causes. Cause-jumping is a serious temptation when

examining any problem, and must be strongly resisted. Managers can often be too close to a situation to be able to stand back and search for causes; there is also the inevitable temptation to assume that a cause that applied last time to a similar problem must be the cause of the present problem.

When possible causes have been suggested, it is best to follow a rigorous questioning process asking of each, 'If this is the cause, does it explain why *each* happening is as it is, and why problems do not exist in similar areas?'

In the manufacturing example above, the delivery problems suffered by small accounts (North) could be traced to the distribution company used for this area and not for the other deliveries. The after-sales service problem was traced to lack of an adequate system of control of service engineers' visits. In the bus company example, the private hire business problems stemmed from inadequate management from a promoted inspector who did not understand the needs of this sector. Staff problems stemmed from a total lack of training in customer service skills coupled with lack of management attention to this area.

Solutions. In general terms, solutions are likely to be found by considering the following types of option:

- Abandon the market segment or service provision that has problems.
- Improve systems or procedures.
- Train staff, perhaps customers.
- Motivate staff by improved status, bonus payments, etc.
- Invest in new equipment or hardware.
- Change staff or sub-contractors.
- Reduce over-servicing to the level required by customers.
- Use high-level standard of service as basis for major promotional/public relations initiative.

The temptation to grasp apparently easy options (such as abandoning segments or services, or investing in new equipment) before possibly more cost-effective solutions have been examined will always be hard but necessary to resist.

Decisions will be taken against a background of cost, although this will not be the whole picture.

For most options, capital and running costs are likely to be far easier to forecast than changes in revenue.

Costs of each separate major element in the plan should be considered under two heads: the set-up, or what may be thought of as the capital costs of an improvement, and the continuing, or running costs.

Set-up costs. These may arise under headings such as:

- Consultant fees (if used)
- New equipment or machinery
- Furniture
- Alterations to premises
- Initial staff training
- Publicity and public relations
- Printing of manuals, etc
- Recruitment (if additional staff are needed)

These may, in total, be amortised over a suitable period, which will generally not be more than three or four years.

Running costs. These may include:

- Additional staff costs
- Higher inventory-carrying costs
- Premium transport costs
- Regular booster training
- Consumables

Not all options will, of course, increase costs. Improved systems or procedures and abandonment of segments or elements of service will reduce them.

For some options, as for example in action to avoid the occurrence of stock-outs, there may be trade-offs between additional costs incurred (such as higher inventory costs), and lower costs avoided (such as premium transport and special order-processing costs).

Increased revenue. This will often be far harder to estimate with any degree of accuracy.

It may be possible to set up controlled experiments to help assess the revenue effect, if the organisation has several operations which are sufficiently similar. As always in such cases, the experiments will need careful design to eliminate extraneous factors, and may need more time than is available.

In all cases, the comparison to be made will be between the

revenue with and without improvements, *not* a comparison between revenue with improvements and present revenue. With this approach, account will be taken of possible loss of sales if improvements are not made.

In considering the plan as a whole, it will be possible to trade off the benefits from the various courses of action in order to arrive at an optimum overall financial outcome from the resources available.

It may prove impossible to find purely financial justification for some improvements. Training in particular is almost certain to fall into this category. Managerial judgement of the long-term market position with and without action should not be based too narrowly. The decision will in any case be taken not against financial criteria only, but against all aspects of the declared customer service policy and any objectives that have been derived from this.

Staff should be involved in the decision-making. The more fully they have been involved, the greater the chances both that decisions will benefit from their experience, and that full commitment will be gained. It is difficult to get value from improved systems or training without the fullest commitment.

Above all, customers must also be fully involved in the decisions. If the proposed improvements affect a small number of high-value customers, then we will want to discuss them in detail with each customer. If large numbers are involved, we will probably decide to consult them through customer panels or a market survey.

Setting the improvement plan in action
If many changes are planned, or the changes are large and complex, then planning will need care; such things do not happen just because we want them to.

Support from the top. Purposeful change will not take place unless everyone knows, and *really believes* that those in authority in the organisation, company, department, division, sector or whatever unit is involved; the chairman and the board, the chief executive, the managing director, the owner, the boss, the old man, whoever they may be, are behind it. This cannot be achieved by sending round a memo; it requires continuing public involvement at every stage, together with change by example.

Project control. It is usually found most effective if the exercise is regarded as a project under the control of one individual, with sufficient authority to carry it through, reporting at a very high level, possibly to the board.

In this way the problems of lack of time and departmental bias which may arise from using departmental managers can be avoided. Such exercises are sometimes undertaken by committees; an advisory committee may be of great help, but will rarely be the right instrument for achieving major changes.

Phasing. Phasing of the plan will need careful thought, and target dates for each phase must be set. A complex plan in a large organisation may benefit from the setting up of a critical path network from which bar charts may be prepared.

Progress in installing the plan will call for monitoring against defined targets and dates.

Public relations. Many organisations will see from the installation of such a plan as an ideal opportunity for a major public relations and publicity initiative. If we are aiming to give our customers even better service, we must make sure they notice it, and this will not happen without prompting.

Changing attitudes and behaviour: the role of training

For success, the plan is very likely to involve changing attitudes of staff involved. This is one of the hardest tasks of management. Strictly, it is only one element of the plan; in practice, its importance is likely to be so great that it should be considered separately, *provided* that it is linked in all ways to the other elements. To have any hope of genuine and lasting success, there are conditions which must be fulfilled. These include:

- Commitment to the change by those in authority
- Insight into the behaviour that needs changing
- Understanding of the desirable behaviours
- Training
- Support from peer groups
- Continuing feedback and appraisal of performance.

The first of these has already been discussed. The next three are likely to be the role of a carefully designed training programme. The last two are aspects of continuing good management practice.

Insight. This should already have been achieved for the organisation as a whole by the customer service survey, together with analysis of customer complaints.

It may remain for individuals to learn about the effect of their own actions. If this is the case, this is the first task to be undertaken in the non-threatening environment of a specially designed training event.

Training. Some of the most successful and powerful training techniques developed in recent years are in the field of sensitivity training, designed to help us understand our own behaviour and how it is seen by others.

There are many group training techniques, of which the best known and for customer service probably the most useful is role playing. This is particularly valuable because of the insight it can give to the perceptions and motivations of the various parties involved in customer service situations. It is particularly powerful if combined with the use of video equipment with playback facilities.

A number of other established training techniques have been used in the field of customer service training. Notable among these is 'transactional analysis'. In this, interpersonal contacts are regarded as *transactions*, in which each individual adopts, usually subconsciously, the role of 'parent', 'child' or 'adult'. It is thus possible to engage in one of nine sorts of transaction; parent/parent, parent/child, parent/adult, child/parent, child/child, child/adult, adult/parent, adult/child or adult/adult. Which role is adopted will vary according to the personal psychology of each participant in a transaction and the nature and circumstances of the transaction. To engage in an adult/adult transaction is the ideal; failing that, one must recognise both the role one is adopting oneself and the one the other participant is adopting, and make appropriate allowances and adjustments, including the giving of 'strokes' to facilitate the transaction.

A training programme should be arranged for all new starters in any post involving customer contact. Indeed, for any organisation which is serious in its intention to improve its standard of customer service, this must be the one most important and worthwhile action; *no one should be appointed to customer-contact posts at any level unless they have received suitable customer-service training.*

Those organisations which are too small for such programmes to be sensibly arranged at regular intervals can get the same help by making use of public courses arranged by one of the training organisations specialising in this work.

Training cannot be a once-and-for-all happening. Booster training is essential. It refreshes people's memory; it gives opportunities to discuss problems and successes that have been encountered since the original training. It enables techniques to be updated as needs change or thinking is refined. It is easier to give short bursts of booster training in real-life teams, thus producing the benefits of group training and commitment.

There are several training organisations specialising in customer-contact training and which have amassed considerable experience in changing attitudes and behaviour.

There are also many excellent films on the subject of customer service, and several larger organisations have already made their own.

Support from peer groups. No lasting change to individual behaviour can occur if colleagues do not support each other in the change. Ridicule of colleagues is one of the strongest agents affecting behaviour; praise, support and at the very least acquiescence is essential if changes are to occur.

If the plan has been the subject of real consultation throughout, and training has been professionally conducted, there will be the best possible chance of this peer support.

Such support can, in some situations, be enhanced by the formation of *ad hoc* groups of employees under some name such as 'customer service circles'. This approach is modelled on the much better known 'quality circle' technique. Groups meet regularly in working time, monitoring their quality or customer-service performance against pre-arranged targets, analysing the reasons for failure and success and making progress (or lack of it) continuously known within the department or area involved. The degree of useful experience and creativity and the strength of the social pressures generated by such a group can be very great.

If everything else has been done, the plan will now be ready to go.

Monitoring results
If the plan has been set up with full project control, including definition of objectives, target dates and individual responsibility, its progress can be monitored, either by the project manager or an *ad hoc* working group.

Continuing feedback and individual appraisal is an essential part of the techniques of good management. If clear objectives and targets are set, these will continue to provide the basis for assessment, both on an organisational, departmental and individual level.

Starting again

The process described in this book is designed to produce a step improvement in customer service standards. Perhaps sadly, having achieved this, it is not possible to sit back and feel the job is complete.

Customer expectations are continually changing. Society as a whole changes; the racial memory of wartime rationing and austerity is finally exorcised; the age mix of the population alters; the spending power of different sections of society waxes and wanes; the geographical distribution of wealth changes; new ethnic groups have new customer expectations; what was a luxury yesterday becomes an expectation today.

New primary products will generate new service requirements; new materials, research and technologies will bring both new needs and new possibilities.

The service given by competitors will change and improve; the lessons we have taught the industry will be learnt by others.

Our staff, sadly, may be fired, retire, or die; less sadly, they are promoted or move to other organisations. If neither happens, there is a high probability we have all gone stale and need new stimuli, a new shot in the arm.

Nothing can be static in this field; no one can sit back on their laurels and say, 'We've got that one sorted'. Whoever would succeed in customer service must remain eternally alert to new challenges; it is no field for sleeping in. Even to stay at the point we have reached, we shall need to run hard; to keep moving forward, we shall really have to rush.

Thought-starters

1. Has your organisation a strategic plan which covers the customer service area? If not, is there any other mechanism that will ensure it is moving purposefully in the right direction?
2. Do you undertake extensive training in customer service skills? If so, how do you justify the cost? If not, why not?

3. Do you involve staff in decision-making that affects them? If not, do you feel it would be (a) practicable, and (b) helpful, to do so?

Action points

1. Pinpoint problem areas by analysis by service element/ market segment matrices (pages 180-81).
2. Cost all aspects of customer service requiring action and compare with projected revenue (pages 182-4).
3. Produce a written improvement plan, with target dates, budget and allocation of responsibilities for results (pages 184-5).
4. Use plan as the basis of major public relations initiative (page 185).
5. Train all staff involved (pages 185-7).
6. Establish customer service circles (page 187).
7. Monitor results regularly (pages 187-8).

The Top Twenty

BELOW IS A list of action points taken from the rest of the book which are suggested to achieve the quickest improvements in customer service performance.

1. Establish a director or senior executive reporting to the chief executive with full functional responsibility for all aspects of customer service (Chapter 11).
2. Define and publish a customer service policy statement, including complaints policy (Chapters 9/11).
3. Carry out a customer service mini survey (Chapter 13).
4. Train all front-line staff in customer-contact skills (Chapters 3/14).
5. Upgrade front-line staff dress/uniforms (Chapter 10).
6. Introduce disciplines within the sales area to ensure unrealistic delivery promises are not made (Chapters 2/12).
7. Give clear complaints settlement authority to local staff (Chapter 9).
8. Examine all systems for bottlenecks and take action to eliminate them (Chapter 12).
9. Install direct telephone lines for key customer-contact staff (Chapter 8).
10. Set up an order-status hotline and a procedure to advise customers as soon as likely delays become known (Chapter 6).
11. Check export terms of trade and revise, if necessary, to 'delivered' in local currency (Chapter 2).
12. Produce and use personalised packing slips (Chapter 6).
13. Set up exchange visits with regular customers for all customer-contact staff (Chapters 6/12).

14. Check and revise all user instruction manuals and leaflets (Chapter 6).
15. Set up and make known a user advice hotline for customers (Chapters 6/11).
16. Start a customer suggestions scheme (Chapter 6).
17. Check signs, notices, layout and furniture of all customer-contact areas from customer's angle (Chapter 10).
18. Organise a customer open day or days (Chapters 6/12).
19. Set up contingency plans for crisis service (Chapter 12).
20. Produce and implement a comprehensive improvement plan, with targets, dates, budget, and allocated responsibility for results (Chapter 14).

Bibliography

Armistead, Colin G, and Clark, Graham (1992) *Customer service and support: Implementing effective strategies*, Pitman in association with the Financial Times, London.

Christopher, Martin (1992) *Customer service planner*, Butterworth Heinemann, Oxford.

Christopher, Martin, Payne, Adrian and Ballantyne, David (1991) *Relationship marketing: Bringing quality customer service and marketing together*, Butterworth Heinemann in association with the Chartered Institute of Marketing, Oxford.

Gerson, Richard R (1993) *Keeping customers for life*, Kogan Page, London.

Hopson, Dr Barrie, and Scally, Mike (1991) *12 steps to success through service*, Mercury Books, London.

Horovitz, Jacques, and Panak, Michael Jurgens (1991) *Total customer satisfaction: Lessons from 50 companies with top quality customer service*, Pitman in association with the Financial Times, London.

Lynch, James J (1992) *The psychology of customer care: A revolutionary approach*, Macmillan, Basingstoke.

Newby, Tony (1992) *How to design and deliver quality service training*, Kogan Page in association with the Institute of Training and Development, London.

Index